About the Book

Hockey has been called "the coolest game on earth," and there are now professional teams in all parts of the U.S., even in the Sun Belt. Once an exclusively male sport, it's now also played by women—not only at the high-school and college level but as a medal sport at the Olympics. This book provides an overview of the game, explaining the basic rules and equipment, methods of scoring, hockey words and terms, and the skills, abilities and tactics needed to succeed. It describes the professional organizations in the U.S. and abroad, as well as international competitions, and profiles some outstanding players both past and present.

For spectators as well as players, ice hockey offers thrills and excitement. Above, fans of the Detroit Red Wings celebrate a goal scored by Paul Coffey at Detroit's Joe Louis Arena. (Wide World)

ALL ABOUT
HOCKEY

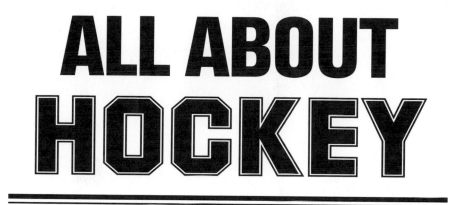

George Sullivan

Illustrated with photographs and diagrams

G. P. Putnam's Sons   New York

G. P. Putnam's Sons, a division of The Putnam & Grosset Group,
345 Hudson Street, New York, NY 10014.
G. P. Putnam's Sons, Reg. U.S. Pat. & Tm. Off.
Published simultaneously in Canada
Book designed by Marikka Tamura
Text set in Caledonia

Library of Congress Cataloging-in-Publication Data
Sullivan, George
All about hockey / George Sullivan;
illustrated with photographs and diagrams.
p. cm.
Includes bibliographical references (p. 120),
Summary: An introduction to the sport of ice hockey, including its history,
equipment, techniques, terminology, rules, and players.
1. Hockey—juvenile literature. 2. Hockey—History—
Juvenile literature. [1. Hockey.] I. Title. GV847.25.S93 1998
796.962ædc21   97-38125   CIP   AC

ISBN 0-399-23172-2 (hardcover)
1 3 5 7 9 10 8 6 4 2
ISBN 0-399-23173-0 (paperback)
1 3 5 7 9 10 8 6 4 2
First Impression

The author is grateful to many individuals and professional and amateur teams who contributed information and photographs for use in this book. Special thanks are due Jessica Buckingham, captain, and Nancy Mace, Tina Fetner, and Gail Schlentz of the New York Comets; Andy Mass and Nick Mider, and artist Patrick Calkins.

Contents

1

The Cool Sport

Ice hockey is a game of lightning-fast action and rough-and-tumble contact, thrilling to play and a treat to watch. "The coolest game on earth" is what the National Hockey League calls it.

Ice hockey had its beginnings in Canada, with the idea for the game coming from the older sport of field hockey. British soldiers in Kingston, Ontario, first played ice hockey during the 1850s.

The game was introduced to the United States in 1895, according to most historians. But at the time in the United States, interest was merely regional, limited pretty much to the Northeast and Upper Midwest. And it was seasonal, since people skated only in the winter, when ponds and lakes were frozen solid.

George C. Flunk is not a member of any hockey hall of

Hockey is said to be related to shinny, a game played in the northeastern United States in the 1880s and 1890s. (New York Public Library)

fame, but perhaps he should be. Flunk was an ice engineer who built the first indoor rinks of artificial ice. These indoor rinks helped Americans overcome the problem they had with ice hockey as a cold-weather sport.

Thanks to Flunk's invention, interest in the game grew steadily. In recent years, hockey's popularity has reached new levels.

The increased popularity resulted at least in part from an expansion program launched by the National Hockey League (NHL), hockey's major professional league. New teams in Florida—the Florida Panthers, based in Miami, and the Tampa Bay Lightning—and California franchises such as the San Jose Sharks, Anaheim Mighty Ducks, and Los Angeles Kings opened up the Sunbelt to the game. Dallas and Phoenix have teams, too. "We're not just a cold-weather sport any-more," NHL commissioner Gary Bettman was able to say.

Beginning in the mid-1990s, telecasts of NHL games featured clever electronic gimmickry to help boost fan interest. The Fox network put a "goalcam" inside the net and electronically altered the puck so that it glowed red or blue on the screen, making it easier to see when it was zipping along at high speeds.

But the most notable recent advance in hockey has nothing to do with pucks that glow or the fact that pro hockey is now played in Florida and California. The biggest change is the number of women that now play the sport.

Up until fairly recent times, hockey was as male-dominated

Hockey action during a National Hockey League playoff game. Pittsburgh's Eddie Olczyk crashes into Philadelphia goalie Garth Snow and Flyers defensemen in a goal-scoring attempt that failed. (Wide World)

as pro football and heavyweight boxing. Not anymore. Beginning in the late 1980s, the women's game began to display astonishing growth. In 1994, Minnesota became the first state to offer women's hockey as a varsity sport on a high-school level. By 1997, sixty-seven teams were registered to play.

Goalie Laurie Belliveau of Manchester, Massachusetts, quit figure skating to play hockey. At Yale University, she set the school record for career saves. (Yale University; Steve Conn)

College hockey for women has also grown by leaps and bounds. There are now dozens of varsity programs for women.

Players are drawn from the college ranks to form the American team that competes in the Women's World Ice Hockey Championships, first held in 1990. (In each of the four tournaments since that date, the American women have been silver medalists. Every time, the gold has gone to the Canadians.)

At the 1998 Winter Olympic Games in Nagano, Japan, women's hockey was a medal sport for the first time. Besides Canada and the United States, the six-team women's field included China, Finland, Sweden, and Japan.

Even professional hockey has felt the presence of women. In 1993, Manon Rheaume broke pro hockey's gender barrier when she started in goal for the Atlanta Knights of the International Hockey League. Rheaume was originally signed in 1992 by Atlanta's parent club, the Tampa Bay Lightning of the NHL, for whom she played several exhibition games.

The women's game is less physical than the men's. There's more deliberation, more time spent setting up plays. There's also a penalty for deliberate checking, for skating into someone. "Instead of checking," says one player, "you skate an opponent off the puck, like brushing someone aside." The women's game has the same penalties for tripping, slashing, hooking, and other of the game's misdeeds.

"The women have lesser egos," John Marchetti, a pioneer of women's hockey and head coach at Providence College, told *The New York Times*. "They are much more into the team concept. You won't find women skaters thinking about their own statistics, about pro scouts who might be in the stands, or where they suspect they'll get drafted."

In-line skating, often referred to as Rollerblading after a well-known brand of skates, which has been called "the sport of the '90s," has also helped ice hockey to grow. Introduced during the 1980s, Rollerblading is enormously popular today. No one knows for sure how many Rollerbladers there are. It's like trying to count the number of people who use the Internet or eat pasta. There are millions and millions of them.

They go blading not only for fun and exercise. They skate-race and stunt-skate. They also form Rollerblade hockey teams and leagues. In San Jose, California, a Rollerblade hockey program, supported by the NHL, involves 50,000 kids.

   Whether it's played on wheels on city streets or on blades on glass-smooth ice, hockey itself hasn't changed. It remains a game of speed, color, and occasional violence, the basic reasons more people are playing it and watching it than ever before in history.

Basic Rules

Every hockey fan understands the meaning of those red and blue lines drawn across the ice and knows the definition of such terms as the "crease" and "icing the puck." But if you're a newcomer to the sport, you may not understand all of the playing rules and the words and phrases that they include. The pages that follow explain the most important of them.

Scoring

A goal is scored when the hard rubber disk called the puck crosses the goal line and enters the 4-foot-by-6-foot opening in front of the goal cage. It must *cross* the line. If any part of the puck remains on the goal line, no goal is scored. It doesn't matter if the puck gets deflected off a goalpost, crossbar, or a player, whether that player happens to be the shooter's teammate or not.

One exception: If the puck is deflected into the net by an official, no goal is scored.

In front of the goal cage, there's a light blue semicircle. Called the goal crease, it's forbidden territory for the attacking team. If a member of the attacking team should happen to be in the crease when the puck crosses the goal line, the goal does not count.

Playing Time

In professional hockey, games are divided into three 20-minute periods, broken by two 18-minute intermissions. During intermissions, the ice is resurfaced—skimmed, sprayed, and frozen—by a four-wheeled machine called a Zamboni.

Only actual playing time counts in timing a game. Anytime play stops—when there's a violation of the rules, for instance—the clock also stops.

In the NHL regular season, when the three periods of play have been completed and the score is tied, teams continue to play until one team scores. This period of overtime play lasts a maximum of 5 minutes. If neither team scores during that time, the game ends in a tie.

In NHL playoff competition, there can be no ties. If the score is tied at the end of three periods, teams continue to play additional 20-minute overtime periods until one team scores.

During the regular season, each victory and each tie contributes to a team's "points." League standings are based on these points, with each win counting as 2 points and each tie as 1 point. Thus, a team with 48 wins and 3 ties has earned 99 points.

The Rink

A hockey rink is 200 feet long and 85 feet wide. While some rinks are smaller, such as the Marine Midland Arena, home of the Buffalo Sabres, 200' × 85' is considered the standard.

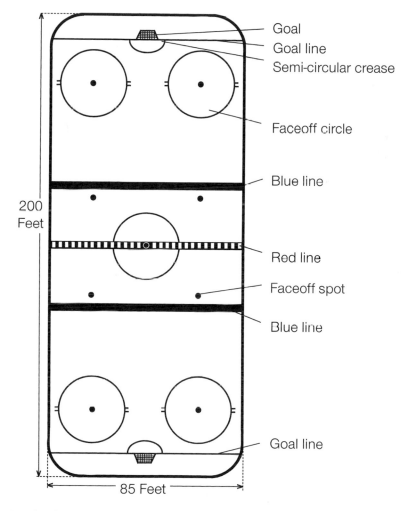

The standard hockey rink.

A low, white wooden wall, 40 to 48 inches in height, called the "boards," surrounds the rink. In the NHL and at other professional rinks, a second wall of shatterproof clear plastic extends above the boards. This is referred to as the "glass."

Two blue lines, each a foot wide, divide the playing surface into three zones that are approximately equal in size. These are called the defending zone, the neutral zone, and the attacking zone. Obviously, one team's defending zone is the opposition team's attacking zone.

The distance from a goal to the nearer blue line is always 60 feet. The distance between the two blue lines varies with the size of the rink, but in the NHL the standard distance is 60 feet. The distance from each goal line to the boards at the rink end is 10 feet.

In professional hockey (but not in high-school or college play), there is also a foot-wide centerline. Red in color, it divides the neutral zone (and the entire rink) in half. It's called the red line.

Penalty Box

Directly across the ice from each team's players' bench is the team's penalty box. Players must sit in the penalty box when guilty of certain rule violations (see Chapter 6).

Facing Off

A face-off is used to begin each game and to restart play after it has been stopped. In a face-off, an official drops the

In face-off action, Wayne Gretzky (left), a member of the St. Louis Blues at the time, squares off against Ray Ferraro of the Los Angeles Kings. (Wide World)

puck between the sticks of two opposing players. Each tries to slap it to a teammate or toward the opposition goal.

Marked on the ice are five red face-off circles, each 30 feet in diameter. One is at the center of the rink; the other four are situated at the four rink corners.

Four other face-off areas are designated by red dots. These are located near the center of the rink, with two on each side of the centerline.

Face-offs take place at center ice at the beginning of each period and after every goal. The other circles or the dots are used when play is being resumed following a penalty or other violation of the rules, or when the puck is shot into the stands or one of the benches.

Offside Rules

The reason for the blue lines is to prevent a player from passing the puck from one end of the rink to the other. If there were no restrictions, a couple of players could simply hang around in front of the goal and wait for passes, which could be as long as the rink in length. Hockey would then be very dull, without any need for precision, timing, or team-work.

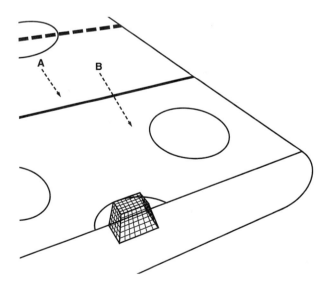

Offside—A team is offside when any member of the attacking team (B) precedes the puck carrier (A) over the defending team's blue line.

So one of hockey's basic rules is that the puck cannot be passed from one zone to another unless the player receiving the puck is "onside"—that is, the receiver must be behind the blue line until the puck passes over it. Or to put it another way: No player on the attacking team may enter the attacking zone ahead of the puck. What must happen is that one member of the attacking team has to carry or shoot the puck across the defending team's blue line before any other player on the attacking team crosses the blue line.

When there's a violation of this rule, an official signals an offside. Play is stopped and a face-off is then held in the neutral zone.

In 1986, in an effort to reduce the number of offside violations and speed play, the NHL introduced what was called the "tag-up rule." It permitted a player to fire the puck into the attacking zone at any time, even if one or more of the player's teammates were past the blue line. All a potential receiver had to do was skate back to the blue line and tag up, like a runner in baseball who goes back to tag third base before attempting to score on a sacrifice fly.

But not long before the opening of the 1996–97 season, the NHL decided to cancel the tag-up rule. The old offside rule was put back into effect.

Offside Pass

Of course, a player is permitted to pass to a teammate anywhere in the same zone. And a player in the defending zone can pass to a teammate in his team's half of the neutral zone.

But an offside violation occurs when a player in the defending zone attempts to pass to a teammate who is beyond the centerline. (Such a pass would cross both the blue line and the centerline.)

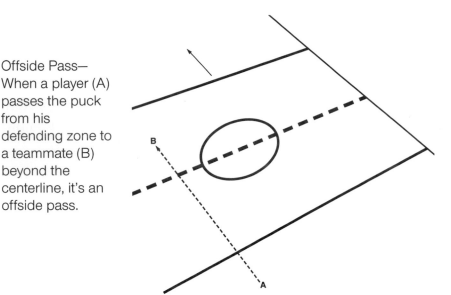

Offside Pass— When a player (A) passes the puck from his defending zone to a teammate (B) beyond the centerline, it's an offside pass.

An official signals an offside. Play is stopped and a face-off is called.

Once the puck is in the neutral zone—that is, between the two blue lines—the centerline no longer matters. Players can pass in either direction, toward the goal under attack or away from it, without any restriction.

To avoid confusion about offside violations, simply remember these two things:

• Any pass into the attacking zone must precede all members of the attacking team.

• Any pass across two lines is illegal.

Icing the Puck

Icing is another common infraction. It's a tactic that teams use when under heavy attack.

Icing is easy to recognize. A thin red goal line runs across the rink at the mouth of each goal. Icing occurs in professional hockey when a defensive player fires the puck from the defending team's half of the ice across the far goal line.

In high-school or college play, icing occurs when a player

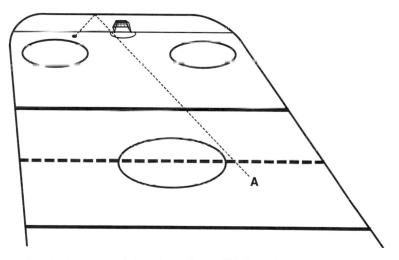

Icing the Puck—When a defensive player (A) fires the puck from the defending team's half of the ice across the far goal line, an icing violation is called.

shoots the puck from his defending zone across both blue lines and the far goal line.

In either case, the penalty is a face-off. It's conducted in the defensive zone of the guilty team.

There are a couple of exceptions to the icing rule. If a team is shorthanded because a player is in the penalty box, the team is allowed to ice the puck as a defensive measure. Also, if the puck should happen to enter the net, icing is not called.

A number of years ago, basketball faced a problem created by the constantly changing size of players, who kept getting taller and taller. Kareem Abdul-Jabbar was one example. Such players would hang close to the basket and wait for passes, then promptly slam the ball through the net. It was very boring. To unclog the middle and create more interest, basketball invented the 3-point shot.

Hockey may try something like that. During the 1990s, some teams have begun clogging the neutral zone with big bodies, with players who use their sticks to hook an opponent from behind, or simply try to hold an opponent in their grasp. The emphasis in hockey has shifted away from dribbling and stickhandling. Speedsters never get a chance to get going.

To help restore a full measure of excitement to the professional game, some rules makers have talked about doing away with hockey's two-line offside rule. This would enable defensemen to make long passes to fast-breaking wingers.

This is an exciting feature of high-school and college hockey. Why not the pros?

Another suggestion is to move the net out from the rear boards by several feet and shrink the neutral zone. This would give offensive players more room to be inventive as playmakers behind the net.

Hockey is not only expanding, it's evolving, constantly changing, and, it is hoped, getting better.

The Officials

The play of a game is supervised by a referee and two linesmen. All three officials wear skates and patrol the ice.

It's the referee who decides nearly all the penalties. The linesmen whistle icing and offside violations and conduct most face-offs.

A goal judge is stationed behind each of the goals. It's the goal judge's job to switch on the red goal light to indicate that the puck has entered the net.

Beginning with the 1991–92 season, the NHL introduced the use of video replays to help referees in disputed-goal situations. A video goal judge was appointed to make the final ruling on such goals.

Other officials include the game timekeeper, who keeps track of actual playing time, stopping the clock whenever a penalty or face-off is called. The penalty timekeeper keeps track of the amount of time each player serves in the penalty box.

Each game is also closely watched by an official scorer. It's his job to record goals scored and the time of each, the names of the scorers, and the names of players to be credited with assists.

Equipment

• *The Puck*—The puck is a hard, black rubber disk that is 1 inch thick and 3 inches in diameter. It weighs from 5½ to 6 ounces.

Pucks are frozen before being used. Otherwise, they can be bouncy.

Gathering frost, frozen pucks await the call to action. (George Sullivan)

• *Sticks*—For years, hockey sticks were made of wood, and only wood. Not anymore. In addition to wood, sticks are now made of fiberglass, graphite, or aluminum.

Some players continue to prefer wood, saying that it gives them a greater "feel" for the puck when they're stickhandling, passing, or shooting. Others choose fiberglass, because it's light in weight yet very strong. Still other players select aluminum—Wayne Gretzky, for one—claiming that it enables them to shoot with greater power.

Make up your own mind; it's largely a matter of personal choice.

Hockey sticks are identified as being either "right" or "left," depending on the way the blade curves. A right-handed shooter and passer—that is, a player whose right hand is lower on the shaft—uses a stick in which the inside of the curve faces forward on forehand shots. The same is true in the case of a left-handed shooter and passer; the curve of the blade faces forward.

Hockey sticks also have different "lies." The lie is the angle between the blade and the shaft.

A lie number is printed on the front of the stick's shaft. These numbers range from 4 to 8. The higher the number, the narrower the angle between the blade and the shaft. The smaller the number, the bigger the angle.

A stick with a low lie number—that is, a stick with a bigger blade-to-shaft angle—puts you at a greater distance from the puck, which should make it easier for you to control it.

A high lie number, indicating a stick with a smaller angle, al-

Stick blades of the New Jersey Devils show different degrees of curve and taping styles. (George Sullivan)

lows you to carry the puck closer to your skates, which can make the puck difficult to control. However, if you skate with your upper body erect, a high-numbered lie might be right for you.

To determine whether a stick has a lie that's appropriate for your skating style, take your normal stance and place your blade on the ice. The blade bottom should be perfectly flat.

If the toe of the blade is elevated, then try a lower-numbered lie. If the heel is off the ice, choose a higher number.

Stick length is another matter to be considered. To determine whether a stick is the right length for you, use the traditional "rule-of-chin" test.

Standing in your stocking feet, hold the stick upright in front of your body with the blade resting on the point of the toe. If the stick is the right length for you, the shaft end should just reach your chin. In the case of a stick that's too long, you can simply saw off the extra inches.

In professional hockey, as players keep getting taller, stick lengths are becoming longer. For 1996–97, NHL rules makers increased the maximum stick length to 63 inches (as measured from the heel to the end of the shaft). For more than a decade, the maximum length had been 60 inches.

The rules also say that the blade of the stick can be no more than 3 inches in width and 12½ inches in length. An exception is the goalie's blade. It is 3½ inches wide and up to 15½ inches in length.

Taping the smooth-finished shaft where you grip it gives you greater control of the stick. Many players also like to create a knob of tape at the end of the shaft. The knob helps to prevent the stick from slipping from your grasp. It also makes it easier for you to pick up the stick should it get knocked to the ice.

Tape the blade, too, even if it's fiberglass, with black electrician's tape. The black tape, contrasting with the brilliance of the ice, makes the blade easier to see, creating a clearer target for your teammates. The tape also strengthens the blade and makes it somewhat less likely that the puck will slide off the blade after you've received a pass.

• *Skates*—Boots for hockey skates are made of a combination of leather and stitched nylon or molded plastic. Not only do plastic boots offer better protection but they're superior in fit and comfort.

No matter what type you choose, be sure to try them on to ensure proper fit. When you go to be fitted, wear the same socks that you wear when skating. The heel should fit snugly into the back of the boot. With the heel firmly in place, the toes should just reach to the end of the boot. Once you've laced the boots, walk around in them. Be sure there's no heel slippage.

Take care of the boots by wiping them dry after use. Blades need special care. Have them sharpened after every four to eight hours of use. Be sure they're hollow ground. This means that the center of each blade will be ground down a little bit deeper than the blade edges. Blades that are hollow ground aid in pushing off, turning, and stopping.

You should also be concerned about the blade radius, a term that refers to the amount of blade that is actually in contact with the ice. (To check the radius, place the blades together, bottom to bottom, and hold them up to the light. The flat area that touches is the radius.)

As a beginning skater, you'll want a radius of about 5 inches. This increases your ability to propel yourself over the ice, and at the same time provides the utmost in stability. A radius of 4 inches, or even 3, helps in cutting and turning.

Forwards normally prefer blades with a shorter radius. Defensemen usually opt for longer-radius blades.

Other Equipment

Hockey helmets are made of shell plastic and lined with foam padding. Safety experts recommend that the padding be at least ⅝ of an inch thick. Otherwise, the wearer risks serious injury. The helmet should be equipped with an eye shield, although not all professional players wear them.

Helmets should be equipped with face masks or clear plastic visors, but most professional players shun them. (George Sullivan)

Elbows are protected with pads made of molded polyethylene lined with foam padding. Shin pads contain molded parts that fit the exact contours of the lower leg. Shoulder pads are designed not only to protect the top of the shoulder but to give the wearer a full range of motion. Hockey gloves protect the hand and wrist without any loss of flexibility and comfort. Hockey pants are padded to protect the hips, kidneys, tailbone, and upper legs.

Get in the habit of wearing all of your equipment whenever you're on the ice, even in practice sessions. Not only does such a policy give you the protection you need, it helps to get you accustomed to what the equipment feels like.

3

Basic Skills

Skating is hockey's vital skill. Unless you can skate fast, turn sharply, and make sudden stops, you can't expect to play hockey well.

Paul Coffey of the Detroit Red Wings was one of pro hockey's best skaters of recent times, and his talent really paid off. Coffey scored more goals than any other defenseman in NHL history. Coffey's secret: skating speed. "You can't stop what you can't catch," it was said of him.

Power Skating

Hockey skating is power skating. With power skating, each skating stroke provides the maximum amount of thrust, with-

Detroit defenseman Paul Coffey celebrates after making his 1,000th assist. (Wide World)

out the loss of balance or maneuverability. Power is generated from the hips, not merely the knees.

Suppose you're going to drive off from the left skate and glide on the right. As you begin the stroke, the left hip and shoulders must turn slightly to the left. As the left skate comes forward, the left hip and shoulder also come forward.

As you stride, lean forward slightly. Be sure that your left leg, the one completing the stride, straightens on each stroke. If you fail to extend the rear leg fully, it's a sign you're not using all of your power. You're not getting your hips into the stroke.

The basic power-skating position also calls for you to keep your chest out and your head up. Keeping your head up helps assure that you're getting a full view of the ice and what's happening in front of you. Whenever you look down at your skates, even if it's just for a second, you become a candidate for a punishing body check.

As you become more experienced at skating, practice lengthening your strides. Get your whole body involved in each one. Your arms and shoulders, important in achieving momentum and helping you to keep your balance, work together with your legs. Learn to make every stride smooth and rhythmic.

Stopping

There are several different ways of stopping, but the two-bladed stop is the most impressive—and the most effective at high speeds. A player speeding along the ice suddenly turns both skates at right angles to the direction in which he's traveling. He stops dead in a shower of shavings.

Always showy, the two-bladed stop is also the most practical method of coming to a quick halt. You simply turn both skates sideways to the direction in which you're skating. Bend the knees, lean back, and push hard on the inside edge of the front skate and the outside edge of the back skate. Really dig into the ice.

In stopping, the idea is to suddenly turn both skates at right angles to the direction in which you're traveling. (George Sullivan)

Turning

When turning sharply, players use crossovers. This is a turning technique that's also common to figure skating, an essential ingredient in almost every routine.

The secret of executing a crossover turn is to lean in the direction of the turn. If you're turning to the left, lean to the left. Lean way over. Bend your left knee and concentrate your weight on the skate's outside edge.

Then lift your right skate over the left. Drive off the right skate. Lift the left skate. Place it down and drive off again. Execute the crossover properly and you'll actually increase your skating speed.

If you do most of your skating at a public rink, where the skaters are likely to move in a counterclockwise direction, it's all left turns. You'll become highly skilled in skating to the left, crossing the right foot over the left. But hockey players have to be skilled in turning in both directions, to the right as well as to the left.

A good drill for achieving turning skill in both directions is to skate a figure eight pattern during your practice sessions. Begin at one end of the rink, skate diagonally toward the other end, execute a 180-degree, turn, then skate diagonally in the other direction, then turn 180 degrees again.

Skating Backward

Defensemen are absolute masters when it comes to skating backward, but it's a skill that every player has to have.

When skating backward, your knees should be bent and your butt kept low. It's something like the position you take when you're about to sit down in a chair.

As you start, drive off the inside edge of one blade, straightening the leg. Shift your weight to the other skate and do the same. You move backward by wiggling, by swinging your hips from one side to the other, pumping your arms and driving off one skate and then the other. Remember to keep your head up.

There are several drills that you can do to sharpen your skating ability. Pro teams often use what's called a "stop-and-back-up" drill.

It goes like this: You and your teammates line up at the

Skating backward, defensemen for the New Jersey Devils (in white jerseys) seek to stave off an offensive thrust by the Los Angeles Kings as the Kings bring the puck over the centerline. (George Sullivan)

goal line. At the sound of the coach's whistle, you break for the center line. As you reach it, the whistle sounds again. You then skate backward to the blue line. At the blue line, the whistle blows and you skate hard for the far blue line. *Whistle!* You skate backward to the centerline. *Whistle!* You skate to the far goal line.

There's no gliding and no coasting during the drill. You drive hard from beginning to end.

Repeating the drill over and over, always pushing yourself, helps to build your endurance as well as your skating ability.

Stickhandling

When you stickhandle, you use your stick to carry the puck along the ice.

How do you hold the stick to do this? It depends—are you a right-handed or left-handed player? A right-handed player puts his or her left hand at the top of the stick, just below the knob. The right hand is 6 or 7 inches lower. With a left-hander, the right hand is closest to the knob.

If you play baseball and you're a right-handed batter, then chances are you'll also be a right-handed hockey player. But if you're unsure whether you're a righty or lefty, take a long-handled broom and try sweeping with it. The position of your hands on the broom indicates how you should grip the hockey stick.

When you first try to stickhandle, don't expect to be able to sweep the puck from side to side, quickly flicking it from the forehand to backhand side of the blade, as you see NHL players do. It takes lots of practice.

Instead, simply keep the puck out in front of you as you skate. Be careful not to let it get too close to your skates. That can cause you to look down, leaving yourself vulnerable to a check. Always keep your head up. Not only does this enable you to see an opponent coming but also you're more likely to spot a teammate who's open for a pass.

Get in the habit of carrying the puck in the middle of your blade. When you feel you're ready to start moving the puck from side to side, keep the sweeps very short, just a few inches. You should be able to "feel" the puck on your stick. Otherwise, you can lose control of the puck.

Stickhandling is a good tactic to use when you're trying to advance the puck through heavy traffic. But there are times when it's not wise to stickhandle. When you're the last member of your team racing up the ice, don't stickhandle. If you should lose the puck, the opposition gets an easy breakaway. Also, don't stickhandle if you can advance the puck by passing it, which is a much faster method of attack.

Passing

Passing and the ability to receive passes are the basis of team play. They're often what make one team superior to another.

Passing in ice hockey is no easy matter. That's because the

passer and the receiver are usually moving, and moving very fast. The pass has to lead the player who is to receive it. This means that you, as the passer, have to be able to keep an eye on the receiver to gauge his or her distance and speed, and then fire the puck accordingly.

One of the game's finest passers ever, Wayne Gretzky (right), here representing Team Canada, eases the puck past Team Sweden's Markus Naslund during World Cup play in 1996. (Wide World)

As this suggests, you must keep your head up when passing. Never look down at the puck.

The Forehand Pass—With the forehand pass, also called the sweep pass, the idea is to simply glide the puck to the receiver. Don't whack it.

When you get set to pass, the puck should be in the middle of your stick blade. Look at the receiver. With the puck a foot or so behind your back skate, sweep the puck toward your target. Shift your weight from your back skate to your front skate.

Be sure to follow through. You should end up with your stick pointing toward the puck.

If the receiver is moving up the ice, you must lead him or her. Pass to the spot where the receiver's stick is going to be when the puck arrives.

While you should deliver the puck with a sweeping motion, you want the pass to be firm and crisp. You want it to travel directly to your teammate's stick as if it were fired from a rifle. You don't want to give an opposing player a chance of intercepting.

The Flip Pass—This is a fairly common variation of the forehand pass. Instead of traveling along the ice, the puck is lifted a few inches into the air. Use the flip pass when an opponent's stick obstructs your passing lane.

To execute a flip pass, use a quick upward wrist snap and a high follow-through. What you're attempting to do is to get the tip of the blade under the puck as you send it on its way.

The Backhand Pass—You also have to be skilled in executing a backhand pass. If you're a right-handed player, a backhand pass is one made from your left side. The back of your top hand moves forward as you execute the pass. Again, you want to sweep the puck, not try to hammer it.

Keep in mind that the backhand pass is going to be more difficult because you're passing from the outside curve of the blade. In addition, your lower hand on the shaft—that is, your power hand—is going to be pulling the stick, not pushing it.

The key to a good backhand pass is to drop your lower hand another 6 inches or so on the stick. Position yourself sideways in the direction in which the puck is going to travel. Look at your target. Send the puck on its way with a sweeping stroke.

Shift your weight from your back skate to your front skate. Follow through.

Receiving Passes

When you're about to receive a pass, keep your stick on the ice and both hands on the stick. If your stick is on the ice, the passer knows that you're ready to receive the puck and you're giving him or her a target. As the passer fires, keep your eye on the puck all the way to your stick. Actually watch the puck hit the blade.

Stay loose. Plan to catch the puck at the center of the blade. Don't tighten your grip. Instead, when the puck hits the blade, loosen your bottom hand so the stick "gives" a little. This cushions the puck, preventing a rebound.

If the pass is ahead of your stick, race as fast as you can and retrieve it. If the pass is behind you, stop, then go and get it. And if the pass is at your feet, block it with your skates and kick it ahead to your stick.

Practice passing and receiving passes. Skate up and down the ice with a teammate, passing the puck back and forth.

Put a traffic cone on the ice near one of the goals. Stick-handle from near the blue line and pass to the cone. Try to hit it on every try.

The Lineup

In hockey's early days, forward passing was not allowed. Only lateral or backward passes were permitted. As a result, the defense ruled. Attacking players trying to work the puck toward the opponent's net were usually overwhelmed by the defense. To spectators, the game was a yawn.

But in 1928–29, to open up the game, the NHL allowed passing in all three zones. (Passing had previously been allowed in only the defending and neutral zones.) No longer did a team have to rely on efficient stickhandlers and speedy skaters to carry the attack. Players could advance the puck by passing it.

Hockey became much more of a team game as a result. This still holds true.

A hockey team is made up of six players—three forwards, two defensemen, and a goalie. But no matter which position you happen to play, playing the game successfully is a matter of working within the team concept.

The forwards are primarily offensive players, skilled in car-

rying a team's attack and scoring goals. Each of the three forwards has a designated position—right wing, center, and left
wing. Together they make up the forward line.

In the past, forwards kept pretty much to their assigned
positions on the ice, with the center in the middle of the line
and the forwards covering their respective wings. But nowadays, there's much more fluid movement among members of
the forward line, more crossing over.

The two defensemen are primarily responsible for preventing the attacking team from scoring. But they are also expected to trigger scoring rushes by passing to the forwards or,
in some cases, even lead the attack and score goals.

The goalie, of course, is a team's last line of defense. Each
goalie has his or her own style, perhaps roaming out to cut
down a shooter's angle or staying close to the goalmouth, lung-
ing and flopping. Whatever one's style, playing goalie is re-
garded as one of the toughest jobs in sports.

Wings and Center

The two wings are positioned on either side of the center.
The right wing is right handed or a right-handed shot; the left
wing is left-handed or a left-handed shot.

A coach doesn't automatically take the team's best shooters
and install them in the forward line. Instead, the line may be
a mix, one that blends together different skills. One wing may
be a gunner, adept at scoring. The other wing may be a digger,
a player who specializes in going into the corners and mix
ing it up with opponents in his eagerness to get the puck.

The center is usually the playmaker. He controls the puck. It's also the center who, because of his skill and experience in stickhandling, takes part in face-offs for the team.

As the team's playmaker, the center is invariably the best passer. Wayne Gretzky of the Rangers and Mario Lemieux of the Penguins were frequently acclaimed as the game's finest passers over the past decade or so. Adam Oates of the Bruins was the equal of Gretzky and Lemieux in his skillfulness as a

As a playmaker, Colorado center Peter Forsberg was among the best in the NHL. Here Forsberg takes the puck down the ice with Don Brashear of the Vancouver Canucks in pursuit. (Wide World)

passer. Oates, however, did not approach Gretzky or Lemieux in terms of scoring ability and thus wasn't as highly praised. For example, in 105 playoff games, Oates had 89 assists but only 32 goals.

For evidence of Oates's greatness as a passer, consider the seasons of 1989–90 through 1991–92, when Oates centered Brett Hull's line in St. Louis. During those seasons, Hull led the league in scoring with 72, 86, and 70 goals. When Oates was traded to the Bruins, Hull's goal-scoring output immediately dropped into the 50s, and he never again managed to attain the totals he had achieved when he had Adam Oates on his left flank.

A team normally has several forward lines, which may differ in character. One may be a scoring line, meant to put the puck in the opponent's net. A second may be more defensive in character and thus more useful against the opposition's scoring line.

A third line might be a holding line. It's put on the ice when a team is ahead in a game. Its mission is to hold the lead.

Defensemen

One defenseman is assigned to protect the left side of his defensive zone; the other defenseman protects the right side.

As this may suggest, defensemen have to be extremely skilled in skating backward. They're usually retreating toward their own goal as the attack comes toward them.

Defensive players also have to be quick on transition—that

Joe Reekie, a lefty shooter, starred as a defenseman for the Washington Capitals. (Washington Capitals)

is, shifting over from defense to offense when their team gains possession of the puck.

Some defensemen are also specialists in taking the puck and going for the opposition goal. They're tough to stop, because such scoring thrusts are usually unexpected.

During the 1990s, defensemen such as Paul Coffey of Philadelphia, Al MacInnis of St. Louis, and the Rangers' Brian Leetch have been noted for their ability to fly in with the puck and surprise a goaltender. They are hailed as offensive defensemen. Leetch was a major factor in New York's Stanley Cup victory in 1994 and was named the most valuable player in the playoffs that year. He won the Norris Trophy as the NHL's best defenseman in 1992 and 1997.

Defenseman Brian Leetch of the New York Rangers was a constant scoring threat. Here he tries to get the puck past goalie Sean Burke of the Hartford Whalers. (Wide World)

Substituting

The three-player forward line normally stays on the ice for from 45 seconds to 1 minute before substitutes are sent in. Defensemen usually play for about 1½ to 2 minutes before being replaced.

In hockey, substitutions are frequently made without any interruption in play, with the players from the bench hurdling over the boards. This is called "changing on the fly."

Coaches change entire lines—the three forwards or the two defensemen—at one time. So the forwards sit on the end of

As the Los Angeles Kings "change on the fly," defenseman Jan Vopat vaults over the boards. (George Sullivan)

the bench closest to their attacking zone. Defensemen sit on the end closest to their defending zone. With such placement, they're able to get into position as quickly as possible.

Changing lines can be tricky. The rules say that the on-coming players cannot leave the bench until the skaters they are replacing are within 5 feet of the bench.

The players on the ice have to pick the right moment to skate for the bench. They don't want to put their team in a weak po-sition, open to attack. They wait until the puck has been cleared and the team is out of danger of being scored upon.

The players on the bench have to be careful, too. If they go over the boards too early, they risk a penalty for having too many players on the ice. The coach is sometimes blamed when such a blunder occurs, but usually it's a player who's at fault.

Goaltenders

The goaltender is the most important player on many teams. The tiniest mistake by a goalie can cost the team a goal. Several of them can cost a game.

In years past, when a young player couldn't skate well, he was often put in the goal. But nowadays the best athletes are goalies.

Teams today recognize the importance of skilled goaltend-ing. NHL teams all have goalie coaches. Goalies themselves are encouraged to work on their conditioning. They work on their legs, improving their ability to move from one side to an-other, and on being able to get up fast after going down.

Goalie used to be a very scary position to play. In days before goalies wore masks, face injuries were not uncommon. Goalies weren't well protected around the shoulders and arms, and frequently suffered deep bruises as a result.

It's different today. The goalie today wears a chest protector that resembles a baseball catcher's chest protector in size and shape. To protect the insides of the arms, elbows, and collarbones, the goalie wears a long-sleeved vest. A goalie's pants have extra padding to protect the inside of the thigh. The goalie also wears leg pads and knee pads.

All goalies now wear masks. The last maskless goaltender was Lorne "Gump" Worsley, who played twenty-one NHL seasons. Not until 1973, when he was attempting a comeback with the Minnesota North Stars, did Worsley wear a mask.

On one hand—normally the left hand if the goalie is right-handed—the goalie wears a catching glove. He wears a blocking glove, called a blocker, on the other hand. The blocker is rectangular in shape and heavily padded, and it is a prime weapon in blocking shots.

The goalie's stick, while generally the shape of the standard hockey stick, has a wider blade and handle. The blade can be 3½ inches wide. The lower portion of the shaft can also be 3½ inches in width. The widened portion can extend up the handle for a distance of 26 inches.

In recent years, goalie sticks are being manufactured with a slight curve to the blade, which helps prevent the puck from rolling off the blade when it is being passed or cleared.

This is important because many goalies are sharp stickhand-

Gump Worsley, whose twenty-one-year career ended in 1974, was the last of the NHL's goalies to go without a mask. (Sports Nostalgia)

lers and particularly adept at passing the puck. During the playoffs in 1997, Martin Brodeur of the Devils won loud applause for *shooting* the puck and scoring a goal for his team.

It happened with 44 seconds remaining in a game against Montreal, with the Devils leading, 4–2. The Canadiens had pulled their goaltender. Brodeur got control of the puck near the left post, then let loose, slamming the puck as hard as he could toward the empty net, some 178 feet away. When it went into the goal, Brodeur jumped with joy. Scoring a goal was a dream come true for him.

Brodeur's feat marked only the second time in playoff history that a goalie had scored. Ron Hextall, with the Philadelphia Flyers, scored in a playoff game in 1989. Only three NHL goalies have scored in regular-season play.

When defending, each goalie has his own style of play. Some keep to the back of the crease and read plays, moving according to what they see. Others move out a little to cut down the shooter's angle.

At one time, most goalies used a stand-up style, seldom dropping to the ice. But a majority of modern-day goalies go down on most shots. As they drop, they fan their legs into a V. This enables them to cover not only the bottom of the net but the lower corners as well. This move is known as the butterfly.

Longtime Montreal goalie Patrick Roy, traded to Colorado in 1995, was a leading practitioner of the butterfly. It was also used by Martin Brodeur, who patterned his style of play after Roy's.

Brodeur also liked to drop down and put the shaft of his stick flat to the ice. "Nothing goes through your stick," Brodeur said.

Goalie Martin Brodeur of the New Jersey Devils limbers up before a game at the Continental Airlines Arena in East Rutherford, New Jersey. (George Sullivan)

Of course, such tactics leave the top of the net unprotected. That's why some coaches don't want their goalies dropping to the ice; they prefer their goaltenders to stay on their feet.

Captains

Usually a team selects a captain from among its players. Identified by the large "C" on the front of his jersey, the captain discusses with the referee any question regarding the rules that might arise during a game.

When the captain is not on the ice, an alternate captain takes over these duties. The alternate captain wears an "A" on the front of his jersey.

With his long reach and quick release, superstar Mario Lemieux led the Pittsburgh Penguins to the NHL championship in 1990–91 and 1991–92. He was the team's captain in 1996–97, his final season with the club. (Wide World)

On Offense

"Just shoot," said Mark Recchi, right wing for the Canadiens. "My junior coach and my dad say that I don't shoot enough. A lot of times you get it on the net, you never know what's going to happen."

Other top scorers say the same thing. The secret to scoring is shooting.

"The most important thing is to have the goalie stop the puck," said Mike Gartner, right wing for the Maple Leafs. "If he makes the save, he makes the save."

Wayne Gretzky agreed. "One hundred percent of the shots that you don't take don't go in," he said.

For most players, scoring is the best part of hockey. And to score, you must shoot and, as the pros advise, shoot often.

The Wrist Shot

This shot is as basic to hockey as smooth ice and two goal cages. Sometimes called the sweep or power shot, the wrist shot is executed with a sweeping action of the stick as you move along the ice. It also involves a quick snap of the wrist at the last moment.

This enables you to get the puck off quickly and shoot hard. And you can be accurate with the shot.

Colorado Avalanche right winger Claude Lemieux shoots on goal during a practice session at McNichols Sports Arena in Denver. (Wide World)

You should be sideways to the net when you're getting ready to shoot. Your feet should be about shoulder-width apart. Bend your knees. Drop your lower hand as low on the shaft as you can go without feeling uncomfortable.

The puck should be a foot or so behind your back skate. Look at your target, the net. Look back at the puck. Then fire—sweeping the puck toward the net with all the power you have.

You get a hard shot by shifting your weight from the back skate to the front skate. It's also vital that you have a powerful wrist snap. You can't expect a hard shot if you keep your wrists straight and stiff.

Be sure to follow through. If you want a high shot—into the net's upper right corner, say—follow through high. For a low shot, follow through low.

The Flip Shot

Suppose the goalie is sprawled out on the ice and there's a frantic scramble in front of the goal. Suddenly, the puck is on your stick.

What do you do?

The flip shot is the answer. With a quick snap of your wrists and high follow-through, flick the puck over the goalie and into the upper half of the net.

There's not much power to the flip shot, and it is usually meant to travel only a few feet. But when a fallen player or loose stick is blocking the net, it's the shot to use.

There's no time to get your feet set. It's a finesse shot. You step up, get the puck on the toe of the blade, and scoop it, lifting it up. It's all in the wrists.

The Slap Shot

The slap shot is to hockey what the home-run swing is to baseball—an all-or-nothing effort. Players and fans love it.

But just as most baseball managers don't like their hitters swinging for the fences, most hockey coaches don't like their players smacking slap shots. The slap shot is not very accurate. The puck can dip or rise; you can never be sure where it's going. In addition, when it's on goal, it's not a hard shot for the goalie to block.

So why use it? Well, the slap shot is an extremely powerful shot, so there is a good chance for a rebound after the goalie makes the initial stop.

The slap shot is often used by defensemen when shooting from the "point." The point is not a particular spot on the ice but a position taken by a defenseman on offense just inside the attacking blue line. In other words, the defenseman is at least 60 feet from the goal. A wrist shot, not traveling nearly as fast, would be intercepted by an opponent or surely blocked by the goalie. A slap shot would be far more likely to find the net.

A star with the Montreal Canadiens and the New York Rangers during the 1950s and 1960s, Bernie "Boom Boom" Geoffrion is credited with inventing the slap shot. (Wide World)

When you attempt a slap shot, the puck should be lying still, about halfway between your skates. The idea is for the stick blade to hit the ice first, an inch or two behind the puck.

Raise the stick into a backswing, bringing it to just above waist level. Be sure that your lower hand is low on the stick. It's the low hand that gives power to the shot.

Look at the net. Then look down at the back of the puck. Cock your wrists. Swing as hard as you can. Really tee off. Shift your weight as you swing. Follow through.

Deking

Anytime you stickhandle down the ice to confront a goalie one-on-one, you should try to get your opponent to commit himself or herself before you make your move. You do this with a fake move, or "deke" (from the word *decoy*).

Colorado's Claude Lemieux, a masterful goal scorer, was successful not only because he could go high or low with the puck but also because he used his tremendous reach to deke the goaltender.

The simplest deke is a body deke. You simply dip your head or shoulder in one direction, and then shoot in the other.

You can also deke with your stick, holding it as if you're going to be shooting in one direction, shifting it, then shooting in the other direction. No matter how you fake, the key element is to get the goalie to commit himself first. Then you make your move. Remember, you have the advantage when you're about to deke, because you *know* the direction in which you really intend to go. The goalie can only guess.

A master at deking the goalie, Claude Lemieux of the Colorado Avalanche scores the first of his two goals against the Red Wings in a conference playoff game in 1997. (Wide World)

Practicing

To practice shooting, line up pucks on the blue line and wrist-shoot them into the net. Practice slap shots from the blue line, too.

You can also arrange pucks in a semicircle about 10 feet in front of the goal line and flip-shoot them into the net.

All players can shoot, but some can shoot with tremendous accuracy. You should work on becoming accurate during your practice sessions.

Mike Bossy of the New York Islanders, who retired in 1987 after a glittering decade-long career, was one of hockey's all-time great scorers.

Once, during a practice session, Bossy revealed his talent as a precision shooter. He noticed that there was a one-inch gap between the goalie's pads and one of the goalposts. When Bossy darted in to take his shot, he changed his follow-through so the puck flipped over on its side while airborne, and it slipped through the tiny opening.

Other NHL shooters are so accurate that they're able to deflect the puck off the crossbar from center ice. Phil Esposito, No. 4 on the all-time scoring list with 717 goals, had this skill.

To improve your accuracy during practice sessions, don't just shoot for the goal itself. Have a more specific target—for example, the upper half of the net, the lower left corner, or the upper right corner.

Shooting Strategy

Of course, the ability to score goals requires much more than the simple knowledge of how to execute a wrist shot or quick flip. Proof of this is the fact that goaltenders are able to stop from 80 to 90 percent of all shots.

Besides shooting skill, there's a mental side to getting the puck past the person in the net. You have to know where to put the puck. You have to have a target.

Keep in mind that most scoring shots are taken from an area in front of the net that is less than 20 feet from the net.

When you shoot from this area—known as the "slot"—you give yourself the opportunity of putting the puck into any one of the four corners of the net.

You also get the chance of making little flip shots on the goal following deflections or rebounds. Be alert for such scoring opportunities by keeping your eyes on the puck and your stick on the ice.

"All my goals are scored ten feet in front of the net," said Dino Ciccarelli, who scored more than 550 goals in a long career with the Detroit Red Wings and several other NHL teams. "I don't score highlight goals. Mine are deflections, rebounds, a couple going in off your legs or your butt."

It makes sense, then, to cut toward the center of the ice whenever you can. When you shift to the left or right, away from the center, you have only one side of the net to target.

From the center of the ice, pick out your target based on these facts:

• The best chance to score comes from the low shot to the goalie's stick side. This is because the goalie can use only his stick or glove to block the shot. He can't catch it; his catching glove is on the other side.

• The next-best opportunity to score is from a low shot on the goalie's catching-glove side. Notice how many goalies carry their gloves high. They want to be able to snare pucks that are headed for the top corner of the net. Therefore, they're sometimes vulnerable to a shot on that side that's 4 to 8 inches off the ice.

A glove save for Dominik Hasek, superstar goalie of the Buffalo Sabres. (Buffalo Sabres/Bill Wippert)

• The third-best scoring opportunity is a shot that's high on the goalie's stick side. Again, this is because the goalie is not able to use his catching glove on that side.

• The poorest opportunity for scoring is a high shot on the goalie's catching-glove side.

Some goalies are more scored upon than others because they leave a gap in between their legs. The space between a goalie's legs is called the "five hole." (So called because the four corners of the net, beginning with the bottom stick-side corner and continuing in a clockwise sequence, are numbered one through four.)

Many players don't pay very much attention to strategic information. They have a favorite spot on the ice, and they usually try to shoot from there. "I score a lot of my goals from the goalie's left; I'm on my forehand," said Geoff Sanderson. A member of the Hartford Whalers at the time, Sanderson was a 42-goal scorer in his second year with the club. "When a shot is coming, I go to that spot. That's where a lot of my goals come from, just hanging out on the goalie's left side."

On the Attack

Normally, it's the center who leads the attack, bringing the puck into the attacking zone. If he has a manpower advantage—three on two, or two on one—the center will try to work the puck toward the goal. But if the center's linemates are covered and the defenders are waiting, the center is likely to "dump" the puck deep into the attacking zone, then race with one of the wings in an attempt to get the rebound off the boards.

The first player to get to the puck usually tangles with the defender. The second player to get there usually goes for the puck.

Meanwhile, the other wing usually takes up a position in the slot, the shooting area that extends 20 to 30 feet out from the goal. There he awaits a pass.

In recent years, power-play strategy has become more and more important in the NHL. A power play occurs after a penalty has been called and one team has at least one player sitting in the penalty box. The other team, which now outnumbers the opposition, puts its best passers and scorers on the ice in an effort to boost its chances of scoring.

Teams have set plays that they use in power-play situations. When a team has an advantage of five players to four players, it usually sets up a perimeter attack, posting shooters at different points around the outside limits of the attacking zone. The basic idea is to move the puck around the perimeter until one of the players gets a chance to shoot.

The four defensive players usually drop back into a boxlike alignment, with two men low and two higher up. The players may stay in the box and defend, forcing the attacking team to shoot through a jumble of arms, legs, and bodies. Or they may act aggressively, with players breaking out of the formation to go for the puck or the puck carrier.

The NHL record for power-play efficiency, established by the Montreal Canadiens in 1977–78, is 31.9. That means that the Canadiens were successful in scoring goals on slightly more than three out of every ten power-play opportunities. Coaches are very happy when their teams achieve a power-play rating of 20 percent or better.

On Defense

Ask any young player, and he or she will quickly admit that playing offense is much more fun than defense. To be able to speed down the ice with the puck toward the goal, to shoot, to score—that's the reason most kids play hockey.

But while defense may not offer the thrills and excitement of taking the puck and ramming it into the opposition net, it's just as important as the offense, perhaps even more important. Take what happened in 1995 when the New Jersey Devils won the Stanley Cup. They did it with their defense.

Anytime an opposition forward would attempt to break the puck out of the defensive zone, the Devils would counterattack with what came to be known as the "neutral-zone trap."

It worked like this: The New Jersey forechecker, usually the center, approaching at an angle, would force the puck carrier toward the boards. There he would be intercepted by a Devils winger. At the same time, the other winger and the two defensemen would overload the middle, cutting off all passing lanes.

The puck carrier had no reasonable options; he was trapped. If he tried knocking the puck along the boards, he risked turning it over or icing it. If he attempted to get the puck to the other defenseman or pass to a forward streaking down the middle, he risked an interception.

Teams often had to return the puck to their defensive zone and try again.

The Devils were a big team. They liked to hit—and hit hard. They used the neutral-zone trap as both a defensive and offensive weapon, converting the many turnovers they caused into goals.

Critics said that the trap was boring. It *was* boring—but it worked.

Checking

Checking is the method used to get the puck away from an opponent. While every player has to be adept at checking, defensemen are expected to be exceptional in the art.

To be effective, checking has to be done with crispness and determination, with what players call "snarl." Defenseman Raymond Bourque of the Bruins, the team's all-time leading scorer, performed with snarl. A teammate, Gord Kluzak, once said of him: "He can slam a guy with a puck into the boards, take the puck away, and start skating up the ice. Most defensemen are going to take either the man or the puck. Ray does both."

There are two main types of checks: the stick check and the body check.

• *The Stick Check*—To execute a stick check, you use your stick to poke or sweep the puck away from an opponent's stick. In either case, the idea is not merely to dislodge the puck from the opponent's stick but also to gain possession of it.

• *The Body Check*—In delivering a body check, you use your shoulder or hip to throw an opponent off balance or halt his progress up the ice.

With an enthusiastic body check, Boston defenseman Ray Bourque drops Radek Bonk of the Ottawa Senators during NHL action in Boston. (Wide World)

The shoulder check is used frequently, especially along the boards. You drive your shoulder into the puck carrier's body, targeting on the chest, pinning him against the boards, then stealing the puck from his stick.

The hip check is more dangerous. You bend at the waist as the puck carrier approaches, then drive into the man, aiming your hip at his midsection. You can also target on his legs. When done right, a hip check can send an opponent somersaulting into the air.

You don't see the hip check much anymore, chiefly because players are bigger and faster. A hip check thrown by a fast-moving 6´3˝, 215-pounder can cause serious injury, especially if delivered below the waist. Some observers expect the NHL to outlaw such checks one day.

Another reason big hits seem to be going the way of cardboard shin guards is that there are many more dazzling, high-speed skaters than ever before playing pro hockey. These players—many of them Europeans—would just as soon not get involved in rowdiness and have no use for hip checks. Hockey is still the roughest team sport around, but it's not as rough as it used to be.

Forechecking

In high-school and college play in the United States, body checks are allowed only in the defending and neutral zones. In the professional ranks and most amateur leagues, body checks can be delivered anywhere on the ice. In women's play, deliberate checking brings a penalty.

In the NHL, much is made of forechecking, the effort by one or more forwards to check an opponent in the opposing team's defensive zone. The idea of forechecking is to bottle up the opposition in their own end of the rink, frustrating their efforts to get an attack started.

Usually only one player, a forward, is assigned the forechecker's role. He's likely to drive the puck carrier into the boards and seek to steal the puck.

When a team is trailing late in a game and needs to get control of the puck, it might try using two forwards as forecheckers. The first crashes the puck carrier into the boards, while the second goes for the puck.

Backchecking

The backcheck is an effort by a team's forwards to cover an attacker that takes place just after the puck has been taken over by the opposition. At the same time, the defensemen are skating back to set up and defend.

Backchecking is not easy; it takes heart. Since the need for backchecking comes at the end of an unsuccessful scoring thrust, the forwards are usually breathing hard and bone weary. Despite their fatigue, they have to spring into action again. Backchecking is a test of character as well as physical strength.

Violations and Penalties

A defenseman gets beaten and the puck carrier breaks into the clear. Suddenly, another defender, coming up from behind, reaches out with his stick, hooks the blade around the puck carrier's shoulder, and jerks him to the ice.

The referee's whistle blares. "Hooking," signals the ref. It's what's called a "minor penalty." It earns the perpetrator 2 minutes in the penalty box. What makes it bad is that while the

Paul Coffey of the Detroit Red Wings hooks Anaheim's David Sacco during a game at the Arrowhead Pond of Anaheim. (Wide World)

guilty party is serving his time, his team must play short-handed—that is, with only four players, plus the goalie.

The speed at which hockey is played and the fact that there is a great deal of physical contact between opposing players makes a penalty system essential to the game. Without it, there would be chaos, with the most violent players in control. Penalties are meant to keep viciousness and brutality in check.

Not all infractions are entirely malicious. Hooking, for instance, is seldom meant to injure a player. It's usually a desperation move, one meant to prevent a goal. Holding, another common penalty, is usually in the same category.

Some incidents that take place on the ice may look like rule infractions, but they may not be. Tripping is one. Tripping often results in a judgment call by the referee. He has to decide whether the player's tumble to the ice was accidental, the result of legal contact, or whether the player was illegally tripped by the stick, hand, elbow, arm, foot, or knee of an opponent. Deliberate tripping is classified as a minor penalty (see below).

Of course, rule violations can be more violent in nature. Slashing, spearing, and high-sticking are often the result of one player losing his temper and lashing out at another. There's no place in hockey for such conduct; it's simply unacceptable.

Penalties range from 2 minutes in the penalty box to removal from the game. No matter how many penalties are assessed, at no time may a team play with fewer than four players (including the goaltender) on the ice. If a third penalty

As the Rangers' Wayne Gretzky goes down, he uses his stick to trip Mark Tinordi of the Washington Capitals. (Wide World)

is called while two teammates are in the penalty box, a sub-
stitue is called upon to replace the guilty player. The third
player's penalty does not begin until the first penalized player
has served his or her penalty.

  There are five kinds of penalties:

  • *Minor Penalties*—These are given for violations such as
those mentioned above—hooking an opponent with a stick or
tripping. They're also assessed for interference, which involves
checking an opponent who does not have the puck; charging,
which is applying a body check after taking two or more steps
toward an opponent; or slashing, which is using one's stick to
hit or attempt to hit an opposing player.

  Slashing can have serious consequences. When a player is
slashed, hands or fingers are often injured. Such an injury can
cause a player to be sidelined for days or months.

  For a player to be guilty of slashing, the stick doesn't actually have to strike the opponent. The penalty can be called if
the referee decides that there was intent to injure.

  In each of these cases, the penalty is 2 minutes in the
penalty box. The team must play shorthanded until the
penalty time is served or until the opposition scores a goal.

  • *Major Penalties*—These are handed out chiefly for fighting, or in cases where one player cuts another, drawing blood.
Spearing, thrusting one's stick at an opponent as if to spear
him, also results in a major penalty.

  Major penalties bring 5 minutes in the penalty box. During
the time the penalty is being served, the penalized team is

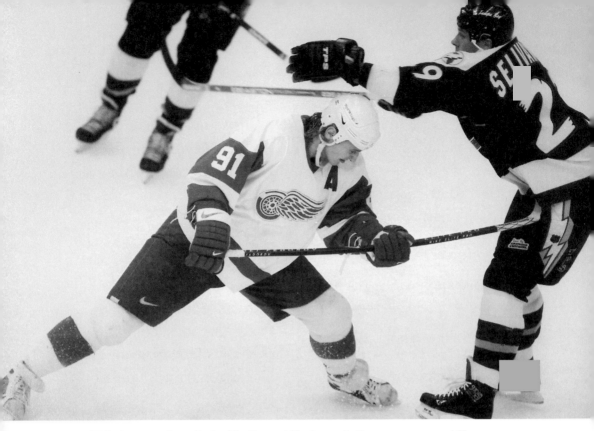

This is spearing. Detroit's Sergei Fedorov is the spearer and Tampa Bay's Alex Selivanov, the victim. (Wide World)

not permitted to play at full strength, no matter how many times the opposition happens to score.

• *Misconduct Penalties*—Deemed even more serious than major penalties, misconduct penalties are given for improper behavior toward an official. Usually such penalties are called for arguing heatedly with an official, using abusive language, or using threatening gestures.

A misconduct penalty brings 10 minutes in the penalty box. The good news is that the player's team doesn't have to play shorthanded; a substitute player can be sent out onto the ice to replace the penalized player.

• *Game Misconduct Penalties*—These are just what the term implies—penalties that call for the suspension of a player for the remainder of the game. Again, a substitute is allowed to replace the offender. In the NHL, a game misconduct penalty also means an automatic fine.

A game misconduct penalty is assessed a player who repeatedly attempts to fight or joins a fight between two other players.

• *Match Penalties*—These are given for deliberately injuring or attempting to injure an opponent. The guilty player is removed for the rest of the game. However, a substitute may replace the guilty player after 5 or 10 minutes, depending on the seriousness of the offense.

Besides these standard penalties, there are also penalty shots, which are always exciting to watch. A player is given the puck at center ice and permitted to skate in alone toward the opposition goal, defended only by the goalkeeper, and take a clear shot. He has one shot, and one shot only; no goal can be scored on a rebound.

Penalty shots are awarded when an attacking player on a breakaway, with no opponent between himself and the goal, is tripped or pulled down from behind and fails to get the puck away.

Hometown fans love to see their team awarded a penalty shot. They realize that about 30 percent of all penalty shots result in goals.

Specialists

Forwards and defensemen are sometimes given assignments beyond their regular duties. Often a player will serve as a penalty killer, and will be sent out onto the ice to frustrate the opposition's attack when the team is shorthanded because one of its players is in the penalty box.

A team's best passers and shooters are put on the ice for the power play, a situation that occurs when the opposition is shorthanded. More and more, games are being decided by power-play goals.

Just about every professional hockey team also has an enforcer, sometimes referred to as a "cop" or "tough guy" or "goon." The enforcer is sent out to balance the scales when a team has been wronged by an opponent or subjected to unwarranted physical punishment.

Most hockey fights have the same script. The enforcer and his adversary throw down their gloves, and for half a minute or so, until a linesman moves to break up the roughhousing, the two punch away at each other. The fans love it, standing and cheering.

Some enforcers take a special joy in their work and look forward to brawling. But enforcing is dangerous work, and all enforcers eventually get hurt.

Their skills may also get buried. For example, a skilled player may end up as his team's cop and never have a chance to develop his skills. Take what happened to Willi Plett, who was the NHL's Rookie of the Year in 1976–77 as a player for the Atlanta Flames. Plett was hailed as a talented forward who also was proficient as a puncher. But coaches tended to overlook Plett's goal-scoring ability and made him a full-time enforcer. After thirteen seasons with four teams, and a total of 2,892 penalty minutes—an average of 3.09 penalty minutes per game—Plett quit pro hockey in disgust.

Hockey has a rich history of notable brawlers. In the 1970s, there was Dave Schultz of the Philadelphia Flyers, one of several hit men who helped earn the team the nickname "Broad Street Bullies" as well as Stanley Cups in 1974 and 1975. A big man, Schultz could be savage during combat, often pulling hair or delivering fierce head butts.

Philadelphia's Dave Schultz was penalized 472 penalty minutes in 1972, a record that still stands. Here he checks the clock from his seat in the penalty box. (Wide World)

Terry O'Reilly of the Boston Bruins, who retired in 1985, was once called "Rocky" on skates. A tough lefty, O'Reilly was the main hammer for the Bruins for nearly fifteen years. When he later coached Boston, the team was looked upon as the roughest in pro hockey.

As a rookie with the Pittsburgh Penguins in 1983, Marty McSorley quickly won a reputation as one of the league's fiercest fighters. Traded to Edmonton in 1986, McSorley played the role of Wayne Gretzky's on-the-ice bodyguard. Do harm to Gretzky and you'd have to deal with McSorley's punches. When Gretzky was traded to Los Angeles, McSorley went along. He happened to be a member of the New York Rangers in 1996 when the club signed Wayne. McSorley never backed away from a brawl and, indeed, seemed to get better the longer the fight lasted.

7

Professional Hockey

Founded in 1917 from an earlier league, the National Hockey League is the major professional league of Canada and the United States. Professional hockey also encompasses several minor-league teams, chiefly the International Hockey League and the American Hockey League, with teams in both Canada and the United States.

The NHL has two conferences, and two divisions in each conference. In past years, the league's conferences and divisions were named to honor well-known figures in hockey history. But these names were changed to more relevant geographic terms before the 1993–94 season.

The cycle of play in the NHL begins early in September with the opening of training camps. During this time, teams practice among themselves and play preseason games against other NHL clubs. Coaches decide which players will make up each team's twenty-member squad and which will be sent to minor-league clubs for additional seasoning.

The regular season opens early in October. Each team plays

eighty-four games—forty-two home games, forty-two away—in a season that lasts 192 days, or until mid-April. There's a three-day break in mid-January for the All-Star Game.

The regular season is followed by four rounds of playoffs, which last two months. The winner of the playoffs is the NHL champion and is awarded the Stanley Cup.

The Stanley Cup is the oldest trophy in professional sports competition. It dates to 1893 and a period when hockey was

NATIONAL HOCKEY LEAGUE*

Eastern Conference

Atlantic Division	Northeast Division	Southeast Division
New Jersey	Boston	Atlanta
New York Islanders	Buffalo	Carolina
New York Rangers	Montreal	Florida
Philadelphia	Ottawa	Tampa Bay
Pittsburgh	Toronto	Washington

Western Conference

Central Division	Northwest Division	Pacific Division
Chicago	Calgary	Anaheim
Columbus	Colorado	Dallas
Detroit	Edmonton	Los Angeles
Nashville	Minnesota	Phoenix
St. Louis	Vancouver	San Jose

* Alignment for the season of 2000–01 and beyond.

becoming a national sport in Canada. Canadian Governor General Frederick Arthur, Lord Stanley of Preston, donated a large silver bowl to be awarded each year to Canada's champion hockey team. At first, the trophy was presented to Canada's amateur hockey champions. NHL teams began competing for the Stanley Cup in 1926.

Teams advance to the playoffs on the basis of the total number of points that each accumulates during the regular season. A team receives 2 points for each win and 1 point for each tie. A team with 22 wins and 3 ties has 47 points.

Team standings are published in daily newspapers and *The Hockey News*, a weekly publication. Besides the total number of points for each team (PTs), each day's standings also lists the number of games each has played (GP), the total number of wins each has accumulated (W), the total number of losses (L), the total number of goals scored by each team, GF ("goals for"), and the total number of goals given up by each, GA ("goals against").

The top eight teams in each conference are eligible for playoff competition. In other words, in 1997–98, when the NHL was made up of twenty-six teams, only ten teams failed to qualify for the playoffs.

The Golden Age

What is called professional hockey's "Golden Age" began with the season of 1942–43 and lasted for twenty-five years. During that time, the NHL was made up of only six teams— in Boston, Chicago, Detroit, New York, Montreal, and Toronto.

Night after night, fans were treated to exceptional hockey. Many observers say that the quality of play was better than at any time in hockey history. And no wonder. The six teams were permitted to dress only twelve skaters for a game, not counting goaltenders. Rosters were limited to fourteen players.

That means that there were fewer than a hundred or so NHL players being produced from Canada's enormous talent pool. Every man in the league could skate, pass, and stickhandle like a master. Goaltending, done almost exclusively by six men, approached perfection.

The word "burnout" hadn't even been invented. Teams played a forty-four-game schedule, which was increased to forty-eight games in 1931–32. (Nowadays, the regular season is eighty-four games in length.)

Without exception, games were played with hard-nosed enthusiasm. Players had no choice. There were countless very talented minor leaguers waiting for an opening. No NHL player could afford even a moment of lackluster play.

All that began to change in 1967. That year the NHL expanded—or exploded—doubling in size. During the next decade, more and more teams were added. By 1980, the NHL had twenty-one clubs in operation.

With all those franchises, players of lesser skill began to appear on team rosters. Play was sometimes sloppy and not very

The Stanley Cup is nearly three feet tall and weighs about thirty-five pounds. (National Hockey League)

exciting. Players would often clutch and grab to offset the skills of superior performers. Instead of relying on artful passing and stickhandling, teams used the strategy of dumping and chasing the puck into the attacking zone.

But a revolution was building. In hockey's Golden Age, with only six teams competing, virtually all players were Canadian. Occasionally an American college player would win a spot on an NHL roster. Whenever it happened, it caused headlines.

But when expansion followed expansion in the National Hockey League, owners and general managers started looking outside Canada for talent. At first they began signing American college players. Then they looked toward Europe.

For many years, the Soviet Union had dominated international hockey, providing impressive teams and gifted players. The NHL began luring players from the Soviet Union to North America.

At first, the flow of players from the Soviet Union amounted to no more than a trickle. But after the Soviet Union broke apart late in 1991, and Russia, Ukraine, Kazakhstan, and several other republics declared their independence, the trickle became a fast-flowing stream. Sweden, Finland, the Czech Republic, and Germany also began to contribute top players to the NHL.

During the 1990s, any list of the best players in the NHL includes a surprising number of Europeans. Among them are Sergei Fedorov, Alex Mogilny, and Pavel Bure of Russia; Jaromir Jagr of the Czech Republic; Peter Forsberg of Sweden; and Teemu Selanne of Sweden.

Headline writers liked to call Detroit's Russian players the "Wizards of Ov." They include center Sergei Fedorov (91), here being congratulated by Viacheslav Fetisov (left) and Vladimir Konstantinov. Their Russian teammates not pictured are Igor Larionov and Vyacheslav Kozlov. (Wide World)

Of course, Canadians are still dominant in the National Hockey League. In 1996–97, the NHL included 396 Canadians, 117 Americans, 49 Russians, 28 Swedes, 23 Czechs, and 11 Finns; also, 3 Germans, 3 Britons, 2 Latvians, one Pole, one

Lithuanian, one North African, and one Korean were on NHL rosters.

Trophies and Awards

Each year as the NHL season draws to a close, individual players and teams receive a variety of trophies and awards that honor outstanding achievement. Besides the ornate hardware, winners also receive a cash award, usually in the amount of $10,000.

The prizes handed out include the following:

• Hart Memorial Trophy—An annual award "to the player adjudged to be the most valuable to his team." In other words, the Hart Trophy is the NHL's MVP award. The winner is selected in a poll of writers in NHL cities conducted by the Professional Hockey Writers' Association.

Center Mario Lemieux of the Pittsburgh Penguins, who retired in 1997, was a frequent winner of the Hart Memorial Trophy, capturing it in 1988, 1993, and 1996. But no player came close to matching Wayne Gretzky's consistency in Hart Trophy competition. Gretzky won the award for eight consecutive seasons beginning in 1980–81, and a ninth time in 1989.

• Art Ross Trophy—Awarded annually "to the player who

The Rangers' Wayne Gretzky, nine-time winner of the Hart Trophy. (Sports Nostalgia)

leads the league in points scored at the end of the regular season." (A player earns one point for each goal he scores and one point for each assist.)

When right wing Jaromir Jagr of the Pittsburgh Penguins won the Ross Trophy in 1995 with 70 points (32 goals, 38 assists), he interrupted a streak of fourteen consecutive seasons in which the award was won by either Wayne Gretzky or Mario Lemieux. (Gretzky won the award in the years 1981–87, and in 1990, 1991, and 1994; Lemieux won it in 1988, 1989, 1992, and 1993.) Jagr's reign as scoring champion lasted only one year. Lemieux captured the Ross Trophy a fifth time in 1996 and a sixth time in 1997.

• Calder Memorial Trophy—This is the NHL's Rookie of the Year Award, presented annually "to the player selected as the most proficient in his first year of competition." The winner is selected in a poll conducted by the Professional Hockey Writers' Association.

Right wing Daniel Alfredsson of the Ottawa Senators was awarded the Calder Trophy in 1996, becoming the second Swedish player to be so honored. Center Peter Forsberg of the Quebec Nordiques, also a Swede, won in 1995.

Other winners have included Martin Brodeur, New Jersey Devils, 1994; Pavel Bure, Vancouver Canucks, 1992; Brian Leetch, New York Rangers, 1989; Mario Lemieux, Pittsburgh Penguins, 1985; and Ray Bourque, Boston Bruins, 1980.

• James Norris Memorial Trophy—An annual award "to the defense player who demonstrates throughout the season the greatest all-around ability in the position." The winner is selected in a poll conducted by the Professional Hockey Writers' Association.

In recent seasons, the Norris Trophy award has been dominated by a trio of exceptional defensemen—Chris Chelios of the Chicago Black Hawks, the winner in 1989, 1993, and 1996; Paul Coffey of the Philadelphia Flyers, who won in

Boston's Ray Bourque, a frequent winner of the James Norris Trophy as the league's best defenseman. (Wide World)

1985, 1986, and 1995; and Ray Bourque of the Boston Bruins, the winner in 1987, 1988, 1990, 1991, and 1994.

• Vezina Trophy—The MVP among goaltenders gets the Vezina Trophy, "awarded annually to the goalkeeper adjudged to be the best at his position." At one time, the Vezina Trophy went to the goalie who allowed the fewest number of goals during the regular season, but since 1982 the selection has been made by the general managers of NHL teams.

When Jim Carey of the Washington Capitals, a native of Dorchester, Massachusetts, won the Vezina Trophy in 1995–96, he became the third goaltender born in the United States to capture the award since 1982. The others were Tom Barrasso of the Buffalo Sabres, the winner in 1984, and John Vanbiesbrouck of the New York Rangers, who won in 1986.

• Lady Byng Memorial Trophy—An annual award "to the player adjudged to have exhibited the best type of sportsmanship and gentlemanly conduct with a high standard of playing ability." The winner is selected in a poll conducted by members of the Professional Hockey Writers' Association.

In terms of sportsmanship, Frank Boucher, who enjoyed a fourteen-year career with Ottawa and the New York Rangers beginning in 1921, was one of the game's all-time greats. Boucher won the Lady Byng award seven times in eight seasons.

• Conn Smythe Trophy—An annual award presented "to the most valuable player for the team in the playoffs." The winner is selected by members of the Professional Hockey Writers' Association following the final playoff game.

The season's MVP among goaltenders wins the Vezina Trophy.
(National Hockey League)

When the Colorado Avalanche won the Stanley Cup in 1996, center Joe Sakic was named as the winner of the Conn Smythe Trophy. He was most deserving, having scored 18 goals in 22 playoff games, including two overtime goals and six game-winning goals.

Minor Leagues

Professional hockey includes not only the National League but six minor leagues in the United States and several others in Canada. Many of these are affiliated with a particular NHL club to provide training and experience for young players.

The International Hockey League, known as the "I" to hockey fans, is the No. 1 minor league in the United States. The league, which celebrated its fiftieth season in 1994–95, boasts nineteen teams, some in big cities such as Chicago, San Antonio, Detroit, and Indianapolis. In the past decade, it has grown in both popularity and prestige.

For years, the IHL and its teams had a scruffy, ragtag character. It began as a bus league, with teams traveling by that means of transportation. The majority of franchises were based in Michigan—in Flint, Kalamazoo, Muskegon, Port Huron, and Saginaw. Milwaukee, Wisconsin, Toledo, Ohio, and Fort Wayne, Indiana, also were league members.

Arenas were small, poorly lighted, and often smoke-filled. Paychecks were tiny. Getting assigned to a team in the International League was almost like being handed a prison sentence.

Change came in 1984. That year the Central Hockey League went out of business and two of its clubs, Salt Lake City and Indianapolis, joined the IHL. With that, the IHL began to prosper.

League executives moved to improve the quality of their

INTERNATIONAL HOCKEY LEAGUE

Eastern Conference

Northeast Division

Cincinnati Cyclones
Detroit Vipers
Grand Rapids Griffins
Orlando Solar Bears
Quebec Rafales

Central Division

Cleveland Lumberjacks
Fort Wayne Komets
Indianapolis Ice
Michigan K-Wings

Western Conference

Midwest Division

Chicago Wolves
Kansas City Blades
Manitoba Moose
Milwaukee Admirals
San Antonio Dragons

Southwest Division

Houston Aeros
Las Vegas Thunder
Long Beach Ice Dogs
Phoenix Roadrunners
Utah Grizzlies

product. Rules against fighting were made stricter. The league adopted a shoot-out in the case of ties so that each game would have a winner.

The American Hockey League, with teams in the northeastern United States and the Maritime Provinces of Canada, had always been hockey's foremost minor league. But by the early 1990s, the IHL was overshadowing the AHL.

Today, the AHL is a developmental league. Each of its eighteen franchises is affiliated with an NHL club.

The IHL is something of a developmental league, too.

AMERICAN HOCKEY LEAGUE

Northern Conference

Canadian Division

Fredericton Canadiens
Hamilton Bulldogs
Saint John Flames
St. John's Maple Leafs

Empire State Division

Adirondack Red Wings
Albany River Rats
Binghamton Rangers
Rochester Americans
Syracuse Crunch

Southern Conference

New England Division

Portland Pirates
Providence Bruins
Springfield Falcons
Worcester Icecats

Mid-Atlantic Division

Baltimore Bandits
Carolina Monarchs
Hershey Bears
Kentucky Thoroughblades
Philadelphia Phantoms

Six of its clubs serve as farm teams for NHL franchises. But thirteen are independent, with the ability to sign any available player.

IHL fans are told that they are going to be entertained from the moment they enter the arena and take their seats. And it's true. Besides the games, there are fireworks and flashy introductions, loud music and zany mascots. It's a circus. In 1994–95, the Las Vegas Thunder offered Manon Rheaume, hockey's first female professional, as the team's third-string goaltender.

But what appeals to the fans the most are the ticket prices.

A family of four can get decent seats for an IHL game, pay for parking, buy refreshments and a couple of souvenirs, and not spend as much as $100. That's about half the amount the same purchases would cost at an NHL arena.

Other minor leagues in the United States include the East Coast Hockey League, the Central Hockey League, the Colonial Hockey League, the Western Pro Hockey League, and the West Coast Hockey League. In Canada, there's the Quebec Hockey League, the Ontario Hockey League, and the Western Hockey League.

Hockey Hall of Fame

For virtually every visitor to the Hockey Hall of Fame in Toronto, the most memorable moments occur in the Bell Great Hall, where double glass walls display portraits and biographies of the more than 300 players, coaches, officials, founders, journalists, and broadcasters who have earned enshrinement. In the center of the architecturally magnificent hall, with its forty-five-foot stained-glass dome, stands the Stanley Cup, flanked by cases containing other renowned awards, including the Vezina Trophy and the Hart Memorial Trophy.

The Bell Great Hall is merely one feature of this museum, educational center, and entertainment complex that houses what is acknowledged to be the world's finest collection of hockey memorabilia and artifacts. In the "History Zone," memorabilia in double-tiered display cases commemorate various eras in hockey's development. In the "Arena Zone," visitors test their hockey knowledge by playing a trivia game against a computer.

"Full Impact Hockey" is another interactive attraction. It pits the challenger against a video of Wayne Gretzky and Mark Messier. With the challenger in the net, the two NHL superstars skate in and fire sponge pucks at full speed through openings in the video screen.

One of the most popular sections of the Hockey Hall of Fame is the "Dressing Room Zone." This takes the form of an exact reproduction of the dressing room used by the Montreal Canadiens at their former home base, the Montreal Forum. Visitors get a behind-the-scenes look at what was once the players' private domain.

There are two theaters for screening hockey films and videos, and a library with 2,500 hockey books and an extensive hockey card collection. There's also a photo archive containing more than 350,000 images.

Established in 1945, the Hockey Hall of Fame was once housed on the grounds of the Canadian National Exhibition in Toronto. In 1993, it was moved to its present site in the heart of Toronto in what was once the Bank of Montreal's Upper Canadian Headquarters. In its first year of operation, the Hockey Hall of Fame attracted more than half a million visitors.

The United States Hockey Hall of Fame

Located in Eveleth, Minnesota, a community that calls itself "The Hockey Capital of the U.S.A.," the U.S. Hockey Hall of Fame honors notable American players, coaches, and administrators. Additions to the roster of enshrinees are made annually.

A mining community in northeastern Minnesota about sixty miles north of Duluth, Eveleth has a special status in hockey because the city has sent more than a dozen players to the NHL, including Frank Brimsek, a legendary goalie with the Boston Bruins during the late 1930s and 1940s. Brimsek also played for the Chicago Black Hawks. Mark Pavelich, who starred on the U.S. gold medal team in the 1980 Olympics, is an Eveleth native.

Visitors to the Hall of Fame are surprised and pleased to learn that cartoonist Charles M. Schulz is one of the approximately ninety enshrinees. Anyone the least bit familiar with "Peanuts" is aware of Schulz's deep affection for the game of hockey.

The World Cup
and Beyond

The headline in the Montreal newspaper said DAMN YANKEES and WOE CANADA. Wayne Gretzky, from Brantford, Ontario, said his native land was "probably a crushed country."

"It's a hard loss to swallow," Gretzky declared. "It's devastating."

Gretzky was referring to the third and deciding game in the championship of the World Cup of Hockey in 1996, won by the United States. The game was played in Canada's Molson Center.

As a hockey nation, the United States had always been overshadowed by Canadian and Russian skaters. The victory of Team USA in the World Cup competition marked a turning point in American hockey history.

Jointly sponsored by the National Hockey League and the NHL's Players' Association, the World Cup tournament in 1996 was the first in hockey history. It matched the world's best players from eight nations. Many of the players

Brett Hull (right), representing Team USA, celebrates a goal with teammate Brian Leetch during the final of the World Cup of Hockey in
Montreal in 1996. (Wide World)

went on to represent their countries in the 1998 Winter Olympics in Japan.

The World Cup competition closely resembled Canada Cup tournaments, which were contested five times between 1976 and 1991. Canada won the competition four times.

World Cup competition is one of the best examples of the vast world of hockey beyond the National Hockey League and minor-league professional play. This universe includes both men's and women's competition in the Olympic Games, flourishing collegiate hockey, and amateur programs in the United States and Canada that involve tens of thousands of men and women and boys and girls.

Team USA in World Cup competition boasted a lineup that could offer stiff competition for the Stanley Cup, if it had played as a unit in the NHL. It included Mike Richter and Brian Leetch of the New York Rangers, and Pat LaFontaine of the Buffalo Sabres.

Team USA was also bolstered by Brett Hull of the Buffalo Sabres, one of the NHL's top scorers. Hull, born in Belleville, Ontario, but whose mother was American, made up his mind to ally himself with the Americans during his days as a college student at Minnesota-Duluth after Canada had rejected him for its national team. Whenever Team USA played in Canadian arenas, Hull heard chants of "TRAI-tor! TRAI-tor!"

Despite the presence of Hull and the other NHL stars, Team USA was not favored to win the World Cup. The

Americans, it was thought, would do well to finish third. Canada and Russia, hockey's two superpowers of the day, were the favorites.

The Canadian team could point with pride to Mark Messier and Wayne Gretzky, both of whom played for the New York Rangers. The Russians had Sergei Fedorov of the Detroit Red Wings, and Pavel Bure and Alexander Mogilny, both members of the Vancouver Canucks. They made up one of the most dazzling lines in hockey history.

A total of eight teams competed in the tournament. The United States, Canada, Russia, and Slovakia formed the North American Pool. Sweden, Finland, the Czech Republic, and Germany made up the European Pool.

The tournament used NHL rules. Most of the officials were from the NHL.

Play was a bit tentative at the start of the competition, but momentum built round by round. Team USA, which seemed faster and better conditioned than its rivals, featured a punishing defense that hit early and often. The team's forwards were quick and tough.

The Americans finished first in the North American bracket, survived the quarterfinals and semifinals, and went on to a two-out-of-three-game championship series against the Canadians, the only other team to have survived the four grueling rounds of competition. The series opened with a 4–3 overtime victory by Canada in Philadelphia. Team USA captured Game 2, 5–2, in Canada.

That set the stage for the concluding game. Fiercely played, it was to include 47 minutes of penalties. In the game's final minutes, Team USA, trailing 2–1, rallied with a stunning 4-goal explosion to sink Canada, 5–2.

In American hockey history, there has been only a small handful of memorable moments. There was the surprising American victory in the 1960 Olympic Games. There was the "Miracle on Ice" in the 1980 Olympics, in which the United States beat the Soviet Union and went on to win the gold. The gallant victory of Team USA in the 1996 World Cup is in that class.

"We all knew this was a team like no other American team," Billy Guerin, a twenty-six-year-old winger from Wilbraham, Massachusetts, who played for the New Jersey Devils, told reporters after the game. "But you have to beat the best to be the best, and we did that."

The Olympic Games in 1998 produced yet another inspirational victory for an American team. But this time it was a women's team.

American women, playing in Nagano, Japan, for the first women's gold medal in Olympic hockey history, defeated Canada, 3–1, in the championship game, a thriller. Afterward, several of the American women said they were inspired to play hockey when they watched the "Miracle on Ice" on television as grade-school girls.

Olympic Games

It's called the "Miracle on Ice." It took place during the 1980 Olympic Games held at Lake Placid, New York.

The United States team that year was made up of young, unknown, unheralded amateurs, averaging just twenty years of age. The team was seeded seventh in the eight-team field, meaning that Sweden and Czechoslovakia, two of the toughest teams, loomed as American opponents in the early rounds. In the final exhibition game, the Americans were soundly beaten by the Soviets, 10–3.

No one gave the Americans any chance of winning the gold. The players themselves were hoping that they might capture a bronze.

The Americans battled hard to earn a tie with Sweden in the opening game. Two nights later, they beat Czechoslovakia. Then Norway, Romania, and West Germany fell to the Americans.

Next, the Americans faced the powerful Soviets in the semifinals. Just the year before, the same Soviet team had defeated the NHL all-stars in the Challenge Cup series held at New York's Madison Square Garden.

Herb Brooks, the U.S. coach, held a meeting before the game. "You were born to be hockey players," he told the team. "You were meant to be here. This moment is yours."

The Soviet team scored first, and then the Americans tied it. The Soviets took the lead again, but with one second left in the first period, forward Mark Johnson scored to make it 2–2.

After the Soviets went ahead a third time in the second period, it was Mark Johnson who tied the game again on a power-play goal in the third period. Mike Eruzione flicked a wrist shot into the Soviet goal to put the American team ahead, 4–3.

Ten minutes remained. The Americans stayed calm and managed to hold off the Soviets. When the horn went off to signal the game's end, the American players hugged and rolled around on the ice. In the locker room afterward, none of them could quite realize what the team had accomplished.

The tournament wasn't over yet. The United States still had to play the Finnish team for the title. Two days after their victory over the Soviets, the Americans beat the Finns, 4–2, although they needed 3 goals in the third period to do it.

As the players celebrated on the ice, thousands of fans stood and waved tiny American flags and sang "God Bless America." It was an unforgettable moment in the history of American sports.

The Soviet Union had dominated Olympic hockey since 1956, when the Soviets had captured their first Olympic gold. They kept winning through the 1960s, 1970s, and 1980s. Only twice in those years had the Soviets missed—in 1960 and 1980. In both instances, it was the U.S. team that frustrated the Soviets.

Mark Johnson is jubilant after scoring the final goal in the USA's 4–2 victory over Finland in the 1980 Olympics. The win earned the Americans Olympic gold. (Wide World)

The American win in 1960 was almost as dramatic as the "Miracle on Ice" in 1980. The Americans began by downing Sweden and Germany with ease, then upset Canada, 2–1, thanks chiefly to goalie Jack McCartan, a twenty-four-year-old infantryman from Fort Carson, Colorado, who made 39 saves. In the semifinals, the United States surprised the experts a second time, defeating the Soviet Union, 3–2.

In the finals against Czechoslovakia, the Americans started slowly and trailed, 4–3, at the end of two periods. It was then that Nikolai Sologubov, the captain of the Soviet team, paid an unexpected visit to the Americans' dressing room. "Oxygen," said Sologubov to the American coach, Jack Riley. "Oxygen."

The American team followed Sologubov's advice, taking whiffs from an oxygen tank before they went out onto the ice for the final period. Refreshed and energized, the Americans scored six goals while holding the opposition scoreless, routing the Czechs, 9–4. The United States had captured its first gold medal in Olympic hockey.

By the 1992 Olympics, the Soviet Union had broken apart. Players representing Russia and other newly independent nations that had once been part of the Soviet Union played on what was called the "Unified Team." The change in name didn't affect the outcome. The Unified Team defeated Canada, 3–1, for the gold.

American hockey players cheer their victory over Canada in the Olympic Games at Squaw Valley, California, in 1960. (Wide World)

By the 1994 Winter Olympics, the reign of the Russians had ended. Canada faced Sweden in the finals that year in what was one of the most exciting games in Olympic hockey history. The teams battled to a 2–2 tie through three periods, then played a scoreless 10-minute overtime period.

A shoot-out was next. The International Olympic Committee had adopted a shoot-out rule before the 1992 Games. It was to take the form of a series of penalty shots, one shooter vs. the goalie, one-on-one.

Each coach selected five players to take alternating shots at the opposition goal. Whichever team had the most goals after each had taken the five shots would be the winner. Amazingly, the five-shot round ended in another tie, settling nothing.

The rules dictated that each team was to continue alternate shooting until a winner was crowned. The first two shooters missed. Twenty-year-old Peter Forsberg, shooting for Sweden, a left-handed shotmaker, then slipped a deft backhander past the Canadian goalie.

Now it was up to Paul Kariya, nineteen, also a left-handed shooter, who later would star with the NHL's Anaheim Mighty Ducks. Kariya skated in at full tilt, veered to his left, and fired. Goalie Tommy Salo got his padded left hand in front of the puck and it rebounded harmlessly away. Because of the miss, Sweden had its first Olympic gold.

Not long after, Forsberg joined the NHL's Quebec Nordiques. He earned the Calder Memorial Trophy in 1994–95 as the NHL's Rookie of the Year. After Quebec

Swedish players celebrate after winning the nation's first gold medal in hockey at Lillehammer in Norway in 1994. (Wide World)

switched to Denver and became the Colorado Avalanche, Forsberg played a major role in the team's Stanley Cup triumph in 1996. For Peter Forsberg, his dazzling Olympic goal forecast the beginning of a glittering career.

In the 1998 Olympics, Sweden was favored by many to repeat its victory, but it didn't happen. The gold medal in 1998 went to the Czech Republic. The Czechs turned back Russia in the championship game to win their first-ever gold.

World Ice Hockey Championships

Since 1924, teams representing various nations have competed for the World Championship. This competition is held annually, except when the Olympic Games are scheduled.

The World Championships are different from World Cup competition, which was first held in 1996 and which is sponsored by the National Hockey League and the NHL Players' Association. The World Championships, on the other hand, are staged by the International Ice Hockey Federation, with headquarters in Zurich, Switzerland.

In the early years, Canada monopolized competition in the World Championships, winning the crown with remarkable consistency. The United States won once, in 1933. During the 1950s, the Soviet Union took over as the dominant team. Between 1963 and 1975, the Soviets were World Champions twelve times. Their dominance continued through the 1980s and into the 1990s, although sometimes the Soviets were successfully challenged by Czechoslovakia and, more recently, by Sweden.

Professional hockey players are permitted to compete in the World Championships. But competition is held in the spring, when NHL teams are playing for the Stanley Cup. This means that the American and Canadian squads are made up mostly of players from NHL teams that failed to make the playoffs.

By contrast, competition for the World Cup is staged late in the summer, before the NHL season has begun. All NHL players are thus able to compete.

In Ottawa in 1990, the IIHF began holding World Championship competition for women. Four tournaments were held through 1997, with the Canadian team winning all four. The United States finished second in each tournament.

After the awards ceremony in 1997, in which the Canadians received their gold medals and the Americans their silvers for the fourth time, Cammi Granato, a forward for Team USA, complained that she was tired of hearing "O, Canada," the Canadian national anthem, which was played at each of the awards ceremonies. "It's just a frustrating sound when we hear that," she said.

Shannon Miller, coach of the Canadian team, had no sympathy for the American women. "They *should* be sick of it," she said. "We had momentum, we won again, and every time they stick their heads up we're going to pound them into the ground."

After the stirring win by the American women in the 1998 Olympic Games, Miller was surely sorry she uttered those words.

College Hockey

In March 1997, when the Fighting Sioux of North Dakota University defeated the Boston University Terriers, 6–4, to capture the National Collegiate Athletic Association's national championship, it marked the fiftieth year of NCAA college competition in ice hockey.

During that half-century, the best American college teams have come from the Northeast and a belt of states stretching west from Michigan that includes Wisconsin, Minnesota, and North Dakota. Other outstanding college teams have represented Colorado and Alaska.

Besides the University of North Dakota and Boston University, the University of Michigan, University of New Hampshire, Clarkson College (in Potsdam, New York), the University of Maine, Lake Superior State University (in Sault Sainte Marie, Michigan), and Michigan State University have produced exceptional college teams in recent years.

At one time, U.S. colleges recruited the vast majority of their players from Canada. But an ever-increasing number of native-born Americans, women as well as men, are playing college hockey.

For male players, a career in professional hockey is sometimes their goal. For women, a place on the U.S. Olympic team represents the ultimate.

As defensive players hurry to get into position, Gerald Tallaire brings the puck out from behind the net for Lake Superior State University, usually one of college hockey's strongest teams. (Lake Superior State University)

College hockey now includes scores of women's teams. Pictured here is Marcie Deering of Brown University. (Brown University; David Silverman)

Amateur Competition

Amateur hockey competition, excluding high-school and college play, is thriving in the United States, Canada, Europe, and many other parts of the world.

In the United States, U.S.A. Hockey controls amateur play. In Canada, amateur hockey is regulated by the Canadian Hockey Association.

Amateur hockey in the United States is growing by leaps and bounds.
These players are members of the New York Comets. (George Sullivan)

Both organizations help in setting age-group classifications
for junior players. They're active in organizing leagues and
tournaments and in sponsoring clinics for coaches and referees. These organizations also maintain relations with international teams and federations.

The Superstars

In the eighty or so years of its existence, the National Hockey League has produced a vast number of exceptional players. Stan Fischler, an icon among hockey writers and broadcasters, once wrote a book called *Hockey's 100: A Personal Ranking of the Best Players in Hockey History.* That was in 1984. More than 200 players are enshrined in the Hockey Hall of Fame in Toronto.

With so many great players, selecting the small handful to be profiled in this section was no easy matter. In addition to the enormous number of players to choose from, there aren't any reliable guidelines to use. For example, it used to be that to score 50 goals in a season was considered quite a feat. Up until 1961, only one player had accomplished it. But nowadays a total of 50 goals in a season is not especially significant.

In making the selections here, impact is what was considered important. Each of the players profiled made deep impressions on the game. Indeed, the effect most had is being felt to this day.

Wayne Gretzky

"The greatest player ever"—that's the way Wayne Gretzky was billed. There are all those NHL records—61 by actual count (which itself is a record). "The Great One," as he is often called, holds the records for the most career goals, most assists, and most points. He also holds the single-season records in each of these categories.

In 1981–82, Gretzky became the first player to score more than 200 points in a season. He scored 92 goals that season, an NHL record that is not likely to be broken in the foreseeable future.

Gretzky won four Stanley Cup championships and was named the league's most valuable player eight times.

Teammates and opposing players spoke of Gretzky's extraordinary ability to anticipate, to perceive what was about to happen on the ice. He actually thought several plays ahead. And he was able to exploit this knowledge with precise passes or shots.

"You have to learn to play with him," Barry Nelson, an ESPN hockey analyst, once told *The New York Times.* "You have to be ready for the puck at any time. He seems to know your next move before you do."

Because of his awesome talents as a playmaker and scorer, Gretzky, a center, helped make hockey big-time. He joined the Indianapolis Racers in 1978 as a seventeen-year-old rookie and switched over to the Edmonton Oilers of the World Hockey Association just one month later. Fans jammed Ed-

Wayne Gretzky was called "the greatest player ever." (Sports Nostalgia)

monton's Northland Arena to watch him perform. The merger of the WHA and the NHL quickly followed.

Edmonton captured the Stanley Cup four times in Gretzky's tenure with the team. Traded to Los Angeles in 1989, he led the Kings to the Stanley Cup finals. More important, he helped boost the popularity of hockey when the sport expanded into the Sunbelt. In Anaheim, San Jose, Tampa Bay, and Miami (home of the Florida Panthers), fans flocked to see the slender, boyish-faced star.

A difficult half a season with the St. Louis Blues followed eight years with the Kings. Before the 1996–97 season, Gretzky joined the New York Rangers.

Wayne Gretzky was born in Brantford, Ontario, on January 26, 1961. From almost the first day that he laced on skates, he was a sensation. He was seventeen and weighed only 161 pounds when he signed his first pro contract.

Mark Messier, Gretzky's teammate at Edmonton (and later at New York), once described what it was like in those days. "He was like Tiger Woods," said Messier in 1997, "if you want an analogy with someone today."

Gretzky has stood the test of time. He was thirty-five years old, a veteran of eighteen NHL seasons, when he signed on with the Rangers for the 1996–97 season.

He quickly proved that he was still a master of working in what had come to be called his "office"—the space directly behind an opponent's net. There, with the puck on his stick, he patiently studied the fierce and frantic action in front of the net. Then he would flick a pass to his left or right or maybe zip the puck to a defenseman breaking in from the point. A couple of times, he even pitched the puck over the top of the net, caroming it off the goalie's back.

Although his skating speed and passing skills had eroded, Gretzky played in every game in his first season with the New York team, scoring 25 goals and making 72 assists. He still ranked as the finest playmaker in the game and hockey's most celebrated player ever.

Bobby Hull

The greatest goal scorer and most electrifying player of his time, Bobby Hull, a left wing, known as the "Golden Jet" for his blond hair and tremendous skating speed, often earned headlines for his achievements on the ice. But nothing he ever did as a scorer or passer caused the excitement that resulted when Hull "jumped" from the Chicago Black Hawks of the National Hockey League to the Winnipeg Jets of the World Hockey Association, an upstart league that began play in 1972.

Hull's popularity was so great that he helped to trigger the NHL expansion from six to twelve teams in 1967, and he was a major factor in the creation of the WHA. By signing with the Jets, Hull gave the league instant credibility.

"Once Bobby signed, we figured that a lot of big-name players would follow," said Gary Davidson, WHA president.

Bobby Hull, the "Golden Jet". (Wide World)

Davidson was right. Following Hull's lead, an army of NHL players switched to the WHA, which merged with the NHL in 1979.

Born in Pointe Anne, Ontario, on January 3, 1939, Hull was "discovered" by the Black Hawks at the age of fourteen while playing junior hockey in Woodstock, Ontario. He was eighteen when he played his first game for the Black Hawks.

Three years later, at age twenty-one, Hull led the league in goals with 39 and in points with 81, becoming the second-youngest player to win the NHL scoring title. (The youngest was Buster Jackson in 1932. Jackson also was twenty-one, but sixteen days Hull's junior.) Hull was the NHL's leading scorer again in 1961–62 and 1965–66.

When the Black Hawks won the Stanley Cup in 1961, Hull, as might be expected, played a vital role.

In his fifth season with the Black Hawks, Hull joined Maurice Richard and Bernie "Boom Boom" Geoffrion as the only players to score 50 goals in a season. Hull, however, became the first to surpass that figure. With 54 goals in 1965–66 and 58 goals in 1968–69, Hull established new highs for the most goals scored in a season.

Hull did most of his scoring with a fearsome slap shot. Its speed was estimated to be as high as 110 miles an hour. "When the puck left his stick," Pittsburgh goalie Les Binkley once told Stan Fischler, "it looked like a sweet pea. Then, as it picked up speed, it looked smaller and smaller. Then you didn't see it anymore."

But Hull was not merely a mighty scorer. He was an excellent all-around player, a deft passer, used on power plays and to kill penalties.

Hull's ability to perform sometimes suffered because of "shadows," players who would be assigned to trip, hook, hold, or slash him. Unlike Gordie Howe, who would seek to destroy any player who struck out at him, or Maurice Richard, who would retaliate in the blink of an eye, Hull tended to accept the hits as a part of the game.

After he joined the WHA's Winnipeg Jets, Hull was often a sensation. During the 1974–75 season, for instance, Hull scored 77 goals in seventy-eight games.

Hull retired in 1978 but returned to competition the following year after the World Hockey Association and the National Hockey League had merged and Winnipeg had become a member of the NHL. In 1980, Hull was traded to the Hartford Whalers. He retired in 1981.

During his NHL career, Hull scored 610 goals in regular-season competition. As a member of the WHA, he scored 303 regular-season goals. That's 913 career goals, a glorious total.

Gordie Howe

Hockey's greatest player until Wayne Gretzky arrived on the scene, Gordie Howe played twenty-five seasons—yes, twenty-five!—with the Detroit Red Wings beginning in 1946–47.

After two years on the sidelines, he returned to the game in 1972–73 to join his sons Mark and Marty with the Houston

Aeros of the World Hockey Association. In 1979–80, Howe played his final season—with the WHA's Hartford Whalers—participating in eighty games and demonstrating that he was still productive. He was fifty-two at the time.

Howe not only outlasted those performers to whom he was often compared, he also outplayed them. Six times he won the Hart Trophy as the league's most valuable player. Six times he led the NHL in scoring. In 1974, at age forty-six, he was, incredibly, named the WHA's Most Valuable Player. No wonder that Howe was known as "Mr. Hockey."

Howe had the talent of making the toughest plays look easy. Effortless excellence was his trademark.

Having very active elbows was another of his well-known traits. Any player who crossed him ended up a victim of an elbow in the face. And some who never crossed him were his victims, too. Howe once said that he played what he called "religious hockey"—it is better to give than to receive.

Gordie Howe was born in Floral, Saskatchewan, on March 31, 1928, the fourth of nine children. His pride and toughness came from his father. "Never take no dirt from nobody," his father told young Gordie, " 'cause they'll keep throwing it at you."

Howe developed a powerful upper body by working for his father on a construction crew during summer vacations. He could pick up a ninety-pound bag of cement with either hand. During the winter, he skated without letup on the frozen

Gordie Howe ended his twenty-six-year NHL career with 801 goals and more than 300 stitches. (Wide World)

ponds that formed in the wheat fields, a hockey stick in his hands.

Howe failed his first tryout in pro hockey. But he kept coming back. In 1946–47, Howe, at eighteen, was a starter for the Red Wings. In his first game, he got into two fights, scored a goal, and skated with the poise of a longtime professional. Beginning in 1949, he started a streak of twenty consecutive seasons in which he finished among the top five scorers in the NHL.

At the time of Howe's retirement following the 1979–80 season, he liked to point out that his career covered all or part of five decades—the 1940s, '50s, '60s, '70s, and '80s.

In 1997, Howe announced that he was planning to add the decade of the '90s to his string by making a comeback with the Syracuse Crunch of the American Hockey League. Howe's debut with the Crunch was set for April 1, one day before his sixty-ninth birthday.

"It's ridiculous," said Maurice "Rocket" Richard, a onetime opponent of Howe's. "He must be crazy."

Because of scheduling problems, Howe never got to fulfill his wish and his comeback plans had to be canceled. Howe fans everywhere, fearful that their hero might have embarrassed himself, breathed a great sigh of relief.

Bobby Orr

Perhaps hockey's greatest defenseman ever, Bobby Orr helped change hockey for all time. Before Orr, it was the defenseman's job to stay back and wait for the attack to come to him. A defenseman was supposed to concentrate on defense.

But the swift and agile Orr, who joined the Boston Bruins in 1966, would carry the puck the length of the ice, then either take the shot himself or pass to a teammate. Orr opened

Bobby Orr is looked upon as the game's greatest defenseman of all time. (Wide World)

up the attacking game to talented defensemen. Among the defensemen of the 1990s who were cast in Orr's mold were Paul Coffey, in the seasons he spent with the Oilers and Penguins, Brian Leetch of the Rangers, and Al MacInnes of the St. Louis Blues. Like Orr, all were playoff MVPs.

With his lightning-fast dashes up the ice, plus his ability to put the puck in the net at critical moments, Orr turned a pitiful Boston team into a winner. In both 1970 and 1972, the Bruins captured the Stanley Cup. In terms of popularity, Orr was the Wayne Gretzky of his time, the game's biggest drawing card.

The NHL record book gives evidence of Orr's impact on the game. During the 1970–71 season, Orr scored 37 goals, a record for defensemen. He eclipsed that record in 1974–75, scoring 46 goals. (Paul Coffey, with 48 goals in 1985–86, now holds the record.)

In 1970–71, Orr also set the NHL record for assists by a defenseman, with 102. It's a record that still stands.

Orr was the league's Most Valuable Player for three consecutive years, from 1970 through 1972. He was named the league's best defenseman a record eight years in a row, from 1968 through 1975.

Bobby Orr was born in Parry Sound, Ontario. He was twelve years old and playing in Gananoque, Ontario, when the Bruins first spotted him. By the time he was sixteen, Orr and his remarkable talents were known all across Canada.

Orr was seventeen when he joined the Bruins at training

camp in the fall of 1966. "I was scared to death," he once recalled. The next season, he was the NHL's Rookie of the Year.

Orr played only twelve years in the NHL, retiring after the season of 1978–79. Bad knees plagued him throughout his career, and he often played in great pain. Had he remained healthy, Orr might have continued playing well into the 1980s.

Maurice Richard

They called him "The Rocket."

"When he's worked up," Frank Selke, managing director of the Montreal Canadiens, once said, "his eyes gleam like headlights. Not a glow but a piercing intensity. Goalies have said he's like a motorcar coming on you at night. He's terrifying."

That was Maurice Richard, the fiery right wing of the Montreal Canadiens from 1942–43 through 1959–60. He was not a pretty skater or a slick playmaker. But if you were an NHL coach and you had to pick one man to play one key game, you couldn't do better than Maurice Richard. As a clutch player and mighty scorer, he had no equals.

Richard (pronounced REE-shard) was the first NHL player to score 50 goals in a season. He did it in 1944–45, when the season was only fifty games in length. He was also the first to score 500 career goals. He ended with 544 regular-season goals.

Richard's potent scoring skills always seemed to reach a peak during playoff competition for the Stanley Cup. In a playoff game against the Maple Leafs in 1944, Richard scored three goals in the second period to break a scoreless tie, and scored two more in the third period. Final score: Montreal 5, Toronto 1. Several players have tied the record of scoring five goals in a playoff contest, but it's never been topped.

The Rocket scored 18 game-winning goals in the playoffs

Maurice Richard (left) and Jean Beliveau of the Montreal Canadiens celebrate after defeating the Boston Bruins, 5–3, to win the Stanley Cup in 1958. (Wide World)

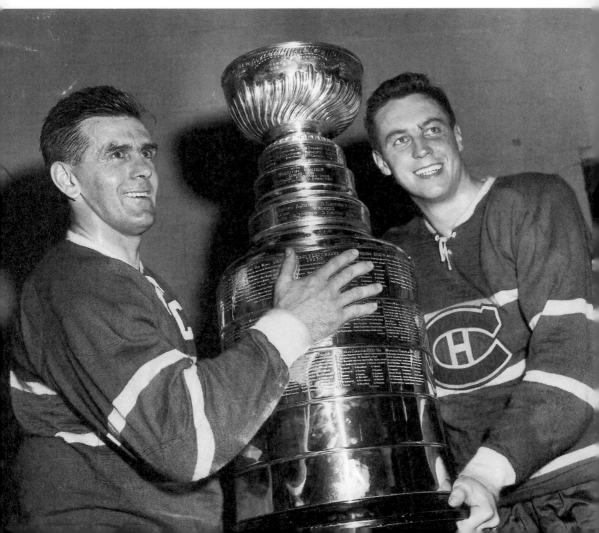

during his career. He also scored six overtime playoff goals, the record.

Helped by Richard at right wing, feeding on passes from center Elmer Lach and later his brother, Henri, the Canadiens became one of the most celebrated teams of all time. Montreal won the Stanley Cup eight times during Richard's years with the team, including five victories in a row from 1956 through 1960.

Maurice Richard was born in Montreal on August 4, 1921. He learned to skate on the frozen Black River near his home. After a career as an amateur player, Richard joined the Canadiens in the fall of 1942.

In time, Richard came to be idolized by the people of Quebec. In the final stages of his career, whenever he would score a goal, the spectators at the Forum would raise the rafters with cheers and applause, and then newspapers, programs, hats, and overshoes would be thrown out onto the ice. The game had to be stopped while attendants removed the debris. Few players have generated such displays of admiration.

Eddie Shore

When the National Hockey League decided to expand south across the border into the United States in 1924, Boston was picked as the first American city to get a franchise. But the Bruins were no credit to the league, finishing in last place in their inaugural season. The next year was not much better.

Then, in 1926, Boston owner Charles F. Adams brought in

several players from the Pacific Coast League after it had folded. Most of the original players were traded, but, fortunately for the Bruins, Adams kept a tall, stocky defenseman with slicked-down dark hair by the name of Eddie Shore.

Tough, absolutely fearless, and an exceptional skater, Shore helped make the Bruins winners. Not only was he skilled in turning aside enemy attacks, he would often take the puck and launch a scoring thrust of his own, a tactic that Bobby Orr would reintroduce several decades later. "The Edmonton Express," Shore was called. (He had played minor-league hockey in Edmonton.)

In 1927–28, with Shore working his magic, the Boston team captured a division title. In the following season, 1928–29, Boston won its first Stanley Cup.

The Boston fans loved Shore. And he also proved an important attraction when the league expanded into New York, Chicago, and Detroit.

Although Shore's skills were such that he was named the NHL's Most Valuable Player four times, in 1933, 1935, 1936, and 1938, his reputation was that of a brawler. While he was quick to hand out punishment, he was also on the receiving end many times. Shore had his jaw broken five times and his nose broken twelve times. He also sustained a fractured hip, back, and collarbone and collected 978 stitches, perhaps the all-time record.

Tough Eddie Shore helped to make the Boston Bruins a winning team. (Wide World)

One of Shore's violent encounters had tragic overtones. In a game against the Maple Leafs in 1933–34, Toronto's Red Horner slammed Shore into the boards. Immediately, Shore moved to strike back. But he picked the wrong man. Mistaking Ace Bailey for Horner, Shore barreled into Bailey from behind, crashing him to the ice. The helmetless Bailey suffered a serious head injury and had to be carried from the ice. His life hung in the balance for days. Although he eventually recovered, Bailey never played hockey again.

The public never let Shore forget the incident. Whenever his name was announced and he skated out onto the ice, boos and hisses rained down on him.

Eddie Shore was born in St. Qu'Appelle-Cupar, Saskatchewan, on November 25, 1902. He was introduced to hockey not as a youngster, but while attending Manitoba Agricultural College in Winnipeg. When his family fell on hard times, Shore quit college and began his pro career, catching on with a minor-league team in western Canada. Shore was twenty-four when he joined the Bruins.

The season of 1939–40 was Shore's last as a player. Midway through the season, he was traded to the New York Americans. Meanwhile, Shore had purchased the Springfield (Massachusetts) Indians of the American Hockey League. His final years were spent directing the fortunes of the Indians.

Hockey Words
and Terms

Attacking Zone—The zone in which the opponent's goal is located. It extends from the goal line to the near blue line. (One team's attacking zone is the other team's defensive zone.)

Backcheck—To check an opponent while skating back toward one's defensive zone.

Bench Penalty—A 2-minute penalty imposed on a team for unnecessary delay of the game, having too many players on the ice, or for using profane language or obscene gestures.

Blocker—The blocking glove the goalie uses to hold the stick.

Blue Line—Either of the 2 foot-wide lines that extend the width of the rink and are located 60 feet from the goal line. The blue lines divide the rink into defensive, attacking, and neutral zones.

Boarding—Driving an opponent into the boards; illegal, resulting in either a major or minor penalty.

Boards—The wooden wall, 40 to 48 inches in height, that encloses the rink.

Body Check—To use one's body to check an opponent.

Breakaway—A play in which a team rushes the opposition goal with more attacking players than there are defenders.

Breakout—An offensive play in which the attacking team attempts to get out of its defensive zone and up the ice.

Butterfly—A technique used by a goalie in which he drops to the ice, fanning his legs into a V.

Center—The player who occupies the middle of the forward line.

Centerline—The red line that divides the rink in half.

Charge—To crash into an opponent; usually illegal, if more than three steps are taken.

Check—To defend against an opponent who has the puck or is going for the puck.

Clear—To send the puck out of one's defensive zone, usually during a power play.

Crease—The semicircle marked off in front of the goal. Only the goalie is permitted in the crease.

Cross-check—An illegal check in which one holds his stick across an opponent's upper body so as to prevent a pass or shot.

Defenseman—One of two players who assist the goalkeeper in seeking to prevent the opposition from scoring.

Defensive Zone—The zone in which the goal a team is defending is located. It extends from the goal line to the near blue line. (One team's defensive zone is the other team's attacking zone.)

Deke—To fake (decoy) an opponent out of position.

Delay of Game—A penalty called against a team for shooting the puck into the stands, pinning the puck against the boards, or otherwise causing an unnecessary stoppage of the game.

Dribble—To control and move the puck on the stick's blade; to stickhandle.

Elbowing—A penalty called for hitting an opponent with an elbow.

Empty-netter—A goal scored after the opposition has pulled its goalie and replaced him with an extra skater.

Face-off—The dropping of the puck between the sticks of two opposing players to start or resume play.

Five Hole—The space between the goalie's legs at which the puck is often aimed.

Forecheck—To check an opponent in his defensive zone.

Freeze the Puck—To pin the puck against the boards with a skate or a stick.

Goalie—The player who guards the goal; also called a goaltender or goalkeeper.

Goal Judge—The official who is stationed directly behind the goal and who signals by means of a red light when a goal has been scored.

Hat Trick—The scoring of three (or more) goals in a game by a single player.

Head-man—To pass the puck ahead to a teammate.

High-sticking—The carrying of one's stick above shoulder level. Calls for a face-off or, if a player is struck, a penalty.

Holding—The act of grabbing or using one's hands or arms to restrict the movement of an opponent; illegal.

Hooking—The act of using one's stick blade to impede the progress of an opponent; illegal.

Icing—The act of sending the puck from behind the center-line to beyond the opponent's blue line, an infraction that is followed by a face-off.

Interference—A penalty called for making bodily contact with an opponent not in possession of the puck.

Kneeing—Using one's knee to check an opponent; illegal.

Lie—The angle between a hockey stick's blade and shaft.

Linesman—One of two officials who make calls on icing and offsides violations and are also empowered to call a minor penalty if a team has too many players on the ice.

Major Penalty—A 5-minute penalty.

Match Penalty—A penalty in which a player is suspended for the remainder of the game.

Minor Penalty—A 2-minute penalty.

Misconduct Penalty—A 10-minute penalty against a player, but one that does not affect the numerical strength of the team.

Neutral Zone—The area of the rink between the two blue lines.

Offside—An infraction called when an attacking player precedes the puck across the blue line into the attacking zone. Play is restarted with a face-off.

Offside Pass—An infraction called when the puck is passed across two or more lines. Play is halted and restarted with a face-off.

Penalty—A punishment for violation of the rules. Usually involves sending guilty player out of the game for a specified number of minutes.

Penalty Box—The off-ice area where a penalized player must remain while serving his penalty.

Penalty Killer—A player who is put on the ice while his team is playing shorthanded to break up opponent's plays, control the puck, and otherwise use up time.

Penalty Shot—A free shot on goal with only the goalie attempting to block it.

Period—One of three 20-minute segments into which a game is divided.

Playmaker—A player, usually the center, who sets up plays that can lead to goals.

Point—A position taken by a defenseman on offense that is just inside the blue line.

Poke Check—A quick thrust of the stick blade to dislodge the puck from the puck carrier's stick.

Power Play—A situation in which one team has a numerical advantage over the opposing team because of a penalty.

Pulling the Goalie—A last-ditch offensive tactic in which a team replaces its goalie with a forward to increase its offensive power.

Red Line—The centerline, the line that divides the rink in half.

Referee—The head official during a game. The referee is responsible for conducting face-offs, awarding goals, and calling rule infractions and assessing penalties.

Roughing—An infraction of the rules that involves shoving or punching.

Save—A successful effort by a goalie in stopping or deflecting the puck.

Screen Shot—A shot on the goal in which the goalie's view of the puck is partly or completely blocked by another player.

Shift—The time a player spends on the ice until replaced by a substitute.

Shoot-out—In Olympic competition, a method of deciding tied games in which five players from each of the two opposing teams take alternating shots at the opposition goal. Whichever team has the most goals at the end of the shoot-out is the winner of the game. If the score is still tied after the five-man shoot-out, each team continues alternate shooting until a goal is scored.

Shorthanded—Describes a team playing with one or more players in the penalty box.

Slap Shot—A hard shot made with a fast-swinging stroke in which the stick blade hits the ice just before striking the puck.

Slash—To swing a stick at an opponent; illegal.

Slot—The shooting area that extends from the net for a distance of about 20 feet toward the blue line.

Spearing—Using the stick as a spear to jab an opponent; illegal, calling for a major penalty.

Stick Check—The use of one's stick to sweep, poke, or hook the puck away from an opponent.

Stickhandle—To control and carry the puck on the blade of one's stick.

Sudden Death—A period of extra play to break a tie. The game ends when one side scores.

Sweep Check—The use of the length of one's stick, flat to the ice, in attempting to dislodge the puck from an opponent's stick.

Tip-in—A goal scored from just outside the goal crease.

Top Shelf—The upper portion of the goal.

Wing—One of two players on the forward line that play on either side of the center.

Zamboni—The machine used to resurface the rink ice.

Some of the more important statistical categories are defined in the pages that follow:

- GP—Total number of games played.
- G—Total number of goals scored.
- A—Total number of assists.
- P—Total number of points (goals plus assists).

• PIM—Total number of minutes a player has accumulate-din serving penalties.

• +/− (plus/minus)—Cited frequently by the media, this statistic helps to measure a player's overall performance during the season. A plus is given each player who is on the ice when his team scores a goal. Teams must be at equal strength or shorthanded when the goal is scored. Power-play goals are not counted.

A minus is given each player who is on the ice when his team gives up a goal. The teams must be at equal strength or shorthanded when the goal is scored.

In the NHL, the best ratings are the 20s and 30s. Naturally, nobody wants to end the season with a negative figure.

A number of statistics apply specifically to goaltenders:

• SO (shutouts)—The total number of games in which the goalie has prevented the opposition from scoring.

• GA (goals against)—The total number of goals that the goalie has allowed.

• GAA (goals against average)—The average number of goals the goalies has allowed per game. During 1996–97, the GAA of all goalies was around 2.80. That meant that a goalie with a GAA below that figure was considered to be among the goaltending elite.

Martin Brodeur of the Devils, who led the team to a Stanley Cup win in 1995, became the second goalie in twenty-two years to finish with a GAA below 2.00 when he registered a 1.88 in 1996–97. The other was Dominik Hasek of the Buffalo Sabres, who posted a 1.95 GAA in 1993–94.

• SA (shots faced)—The total number of shots directed at a goalie.

• SP (save percentage)—The percentage of shots blocked by a goalie. NHL goalies are usually expected to block at least 90 percent of all shots. Dominik Hasek, who made incredible saves, led all goalies in 1996–97 with a save percentage of 93.0.

• Adv. (advantage)—The number of times a team has had a power-play situation.

• TSH (total times shorthanded)

• PGA (power-play goals allowed)—This statistic divided by a team's TSH produces a percentage that measures a team's efficiency in killing penalties. A penalty-killing percentage of 90 or better is excellent.

All-Time Records

Most Seasons—26, Gordie Howe, Detroit, 1946–47 to 1970–71; Hartford, 1979–80

Most Games—1,767, Gordie Howe, Detroit, 1946–47 to 1970–71; Hartford, 1979–80

Most Games, Including Playoffs—1,924, Gordie Howe, Detroit, 1946–47 to 1970–71; Hartford, 1979–80

Most Consecutive Games—964, Doug Jarvis, Montreal, Washington, Hartford, October 8, 1975–October 10, 1987

Most Goals—862, Wayne Gretzky, Edmonton, Los Angeles, St. Louis, New York Rangers

Most Goals, Including Playoffs—984, Wayne Gretzky, Edmonton, Los Angeles, St. Louis, New York Rangers

Most Goals, One Season—92, Wayne Gretzky, Edmonton, 1981–82

Most Goals, One Season, Including Playoffs—100, Wayne Gretzky, Edmonton, 1983–84

Most Goals, One Game—7, Joe Malone, Quebec Bulldogs, January 31, 1920 (vs. Toronto)

Most Goals, One Period—4, Harvey "Busher" Jackson, Toronto, November 20, 1934, at St. Louis (third period)

Most Assists—1,843, Wayne Gretzky, Edmonton, Los Angeles, St. Louis, New York Rangers

Most Assists, Including Playoffs—2,103, Wayne Gretzky, Edmonton, Los Angeles, St. Louis, New York Rangers

Most Assists, One Season—163, Wayne Gretzky, Edmonton, 1985–86

Most Assists, One Season, Including Playoffs—174, Wayne Gretzky, Edmonton, 1985–86

Most Assists, One Game—7, Billy Taylor, Detroit, March 16, 1947 (at Chicago)

Most Assists, One Period—5, Dale Hawerchuk, Winnipeg, March 6, 1984 (at Los Angeles)

Most Points—2,705, Wayne Gretzky, Edmonton, Los Angeles, St. Louis, New York Rangers

Most Points, Including Playoffs—3,087, Wayne Gretzky, Edmonton, Los Angeles, St. Louis, New York Rangers

Most Points, One Season—215, Wayne Gretzky, Edmonton, 1985–86

Most Points, One Season, Including Playoffs—255, Wayne Gretzky, Edmonton, 1984–85

Most Points, One Game—10, Darryl Sittler, Toronto, February 7, 1976 (vs. Boston)

Most Points, One Period—6, Bryan Trottier, New York Islanders, December 23, 1978 (vs. New York Rangers)

Most Power-Play Goals, One Season—34, Tim Kerr, Philadelphia, 1985–86

Most Shorthand Goals, One Season—13, Mario Lemieux, Pittsburgh, 1988–89

Most Overtime Goals, Career—9, Mario Lemieux, Pittsburgh

Most Overtime Assists, Career—12, Wayne Gretzky, Edmonton, Los Angeles, St. Louis, New York Rangers

Most Overtime Points, Career—19, Mario Lemieux, Pittsburgh

Most Shots on Goal, One Season—550, Phil Esposito, Boston 1970–71

Most Penalty Minutes—3,966, Dave Williams, Toronto, Vancouver, Detroit, Los Angeles, Hartford (14 seasons)

Most Penalty Minutes, Including Playoffs—4,421, Dave Williams, Toronto, Vancouver, Detroit, Los Angeles, Hartford (14 seasons)

Most Penalty Minutes, One Season—472, Dave Schultz, Philadelphia, 1974–75

Most Penalties, One Game—10, Chris Nilan, Boston, March 31, 1991 (vs. Hartford)

Most Penalty Minutes, One Game—67, Randy Holt, Los Angeles, March 11, 1979 (vs. Philadelphia)

Additional Resources

WEB SITES

National Hockey League: www.nhl.com
Hockey Hall of Fame: www.hhof.com

ADDITIONAL READING

Brodeur, Denis, and Daniel Daignault. *Goalies: Guardians of the Net*. Toronto: Key Porter Books, 1995.

Chambers, Dave. *Complete Hockey Instruction*. Chicago: Contemporary Books, 1994.

Duplacey, James, editor. *The Annotated Rules of Hockey*. New York: Lyons & Burford, 1996.

Etue, Elizabeth, and Megan K. Williams. *On the Edge: Women Making Hockey History*. Toronto: Second Story Press, 1996.

Falla, Jack. *Sports Illustrated Hockey: Learn to Play the Modern Way*. New York: Sports Illustrated Books, 1994.

Fischler, Stan. *Hockey Stars Speak.* Toronto: Warwick Publishing, 1996.

Hollander, Zander, editor. *Inside Sports: Hockey* (formerly *The Complete Encyclopedia of Hockey*). Detroit: Gale Research, 1997.

Irvin, Dick. *Behind the Bench: Coaches Talk About Life in the NHL.* Toronto: McClelland & Stewart, 1994.

McKinley, Michael. *Hockey Hall of Fame Legends: The Official Book.* Toronto: Viking, 1993.

The National Hockey League, Official Guide and Record Book. Greg Inglis, editor. New York: The National Hockey League, 1996.

Official Rules of In-Line Hockey. Chicago: Triumph Books, 1994.

Official Rules of the NHL. New York: National Hockey League, 1997.

Sullivan, George. *In-Line Skating; A Complete Guide for Beginners.* New York: Cobblehill/Dutton, 1993.

ADDRESSES

American Hockey League
425 Union St.
West Springfield, MA
01089-4108

Canadian Hockey Association
Olympic Saddledome
Calgary, Alberta
T2P 2K8

Hockey Hall of Fame
BCE Place
30 Yonge St.
Toronto, Ontario
M5E 1Y8

International Hockey League
1577 North Woodward
Suite 212
Bloomfield Hills, MI
48303-2820

International Ice Hockey Federation
Todistrasse, 23
CH-8002
Zurich, Switzerland

National Hockey League
1151 Avenue of the Americas
47th Floor
New York, NY
10020-1198

National Hockey League
1800 McGill College Ave.
Suite 2600
Montreal, Quebec
H3A 3J6

National Hockey League
75 International Blvd.
Suite 300
Toronto, Ontario
M9W 6L9

NHL Europe
Signaustrasse 1
8008
Zurich, Switzerland

United States Hockey Hall of Fame
Hat Trick Ave.
P.O. Box 657
Eveleth, MN
55734

U.S.A. Hockey
4965 N. 30th St.
Colorado Springs, CO
80919

Index

Numbers in *italics* refer to illustrations.

155